RELEASED TO SOAR

The Power of Forgiveness

Valecia Tigner, D.D.

Released to Soar: The Power of Forgiveness

Copyright © 2023 by Valecia Tigner, D.D.

All rights reserved. This book or any portion thereof may not be reproduced or used in any manner whatsoever without the express written permission of the publisher except for the use of brief quotations in a book review.

Paperback ISBN: 979-8-9892493-1-2
Ebook ISBN: 979-8-9892493-0-5

Editing: Felicia Murrell

Publishing Assistance: TymmPublishing.com

Contents

INTRODUCTION	V
1. Help Wanted	1
2. Breaking Free from the Past	15
3. Finally, I Know Who I Am	29
4. The Power of Forgiveness	49
5. Overcoming Fear and Anxiety	71
6. The Soaring Life	87
7. The Ultimate Destination	105
CONCLUSION	125
About the Author	129

INTRODUCTION

As the sun rises each morning, so does a new opportunity to embrace the freedom and purpose that is found in Christ. In *Released to Soar*, we will journey together through the highs and lows of my life, discovering how I broke free from the chains that bound me and took flight toward the purpose that God had ordained for me.

With personal accounts of my life stories, along with biblical insights, this book will awaken your heart to the truth that you were created to soar. You were not meant to live a life of captivity, fear, or anxiety. Instead, you were designed to spread your wings and take flight, soaring high above the storms of life like I did.

Through the pages of *Released to Soar*, you will learn how to break free from the limitations that have held you back and step into the fullness of your identity and purpose in Christ. You will be inspired to let go of the past, embrace the present, and look forward with hope and anticipation to the future that God has planned for you.

If you're tired of feeling stuck in life, held back by past mistakes or trapped in a cycle of fear and anxiety, this book is for you.

You'll learn how to:

- Embrace your identity in Christ and live confidently in your calling.

- Break free from negative thought patterns and embrace God's truth.

- Forgive yourself and others and experience true freedom.

- Cultivate a deeper relationship with God and experience His love and grace like never before.

As human beings, we often find ourselves trapped in the cages of our past, limited by our own fears and insecurities. But what if there was a way to break free and soar to new heights of joy, peace, and purpose? In *Released to Soar*, we explore the transformative power of God's love and grace, which have the power to unlock the chains that bind us and set us free to fly. Through inspiring stories, practical advice, and a deep dive into Scripture, this book will help you discover your true identity in Christ and unleash the potential that God has placed within you. So, if you're ready to take flight and live the abundant life that God has planned for you, then join us on this journey of faith and freedom. You were meant to soar, and *Released to Soar* will show you how.

CHAPTER ONE

Help Wanted

Have you ever found yourself struggling with a problem and feeling like there's no way out? Maybe you feel overwhelmed, alone, or lost. As Christians, we often believe that we should be able to handle everything on our own, relying on our faith to see us through. But the truth is, sometimes we need help from others to truly soar.

In this first chapter, we will explore the power of asking for help and reaching for help in correlation to being released to soar. We'll delve into biblical teachings that encourage us to seek out the support of others when we need it, and how this can help us achieve our goals and reach our full potential.

We'll discover the many benefits of seeking help from a Christian perspective and learn how to overcome any shame or embarrassment that may hold us back from asking for the support we need. Whether you're struggling with a personal problem, a difficult relationship, or a challenging situation at work or school, this eBook will provide you with the tools and guidance you need to overcome your obstacles and reach for the sky.

The journey to freedom and soaring begins with asking for help and reaching out to others. This chapter will explore the importance of transparency, humility, and changing our friends, environment, and mindset. By admitting our weaknesses and seeking support from others, we can overcome obstacles and grow in faith.

So, if you're ready to release yourself from the limitations that are holding you back and soar to new heights in your personal and spiritual life, let's dive in!

Ask for Help

In the Bible, we Christians are encouraged to ask for help when we need it, both from God and from other believers. For example, James 5:13-16 says, "Is anyone among you in trouble? Let them pray. Is anyone happy? Let them sing songs of praise. Is anyone among you sick? Let them call the elders of the church to pray over them and anoint them with oil in the name of the Lord. And the prayer offered in faith will make the sick person well; the Lord will raise them up. If they have sinned, they will be forgiven. Therefore, confess your sins to each other and pray for each other so that you may be healed. The prayer of a righteous person is powerful and effective."

Asking for help is an act of humility and recognition that one cannot handle everything on their own. It is a manifestation of faith in God and an acknowledgment of our dependence on Him. We believe that God wants us to help one another and that asking for help is a way to fulfill this commandment.

Asking for help also means being willing to receive it with gratitude and humility. We, Christians, believe that God can use others to bless us and that by receiving help from others, we are also giving them an opportunity to serve and show God's love. Overall, asking for help is a fundamental aspect of our faith and a way to deepen our relationship with God and others.

Transparency

In today's world, it can be easy to hide behind a facade of perfection, especially when it comes to our faith. We may feel pressure to present a polished image of ourselves and our relationship with God, but this can actually hinder our spiritual growth and connection with others.

Transparency, on the other hand, involves honesty, vulnerability, and authenticity. It means being real about our struggles, doubts, and imperfections, and allowing others to see the messy parts of our lives. This may seem scary at first, but the benefits of transparency far outweigh the risks.

Transparency is important because it is closely related to honesty and integrity, which are fundamental values of the faith. The Bible teaches that lying to oneself or others is a sin and can lead to spiritual and emotional harm. Transparency reflects the values of truthfulness and integrity, which are central to the teachings of Jesus Christ. Christians are called to be transparent in their relationships with others, to speak truthfully, and to avoid deceit and manipulation.

One example of the importance of transparency in the Bible can be found in Psalm 51, where David confesses his sin to God and asks for forgiveness. He acknowledges that he has sinned against God and that his wrongdoing has caused him to feel guilt and shame. By being honest with himself and with God, David is able to seek the help he needs to be restored to a right relationship with God.

In addition to seeking forgiveness and restoration, transparency can also help us to grow and develop as individuals. When we are honest with ourselves about our strengths and weaknesses, we can work on improving ourselves and becoming the best versions of ourselves.

We are accountable to God for our thoughts, words, and actions, and we are also accountable to other believers who can help us stay on track and encourage us in our spiritual journey. By being transparent with others, we can build trust, foster deeper relationships, and create a sense of community where we can grow together in our faith.

REACH FOR HELP

The Bible teaches that humans are not meant to go through life alone, and that we are designed for community and relationship with both God and others. In times of trouble or crisis, we are encouraged to turn to God in prayer and seek His help, comfort, and guidance through His word, the Bible. At the same time, we are also called to love and serve one another, to bear one another's burdens, and to offer support and encouragement to those who are struggling. This can take many forms, including acts of kindness, practical assistance, and emotional support.

When we face challenges in life, it can be tempting to try to handle everything on our own. We may feel embarrassed or ashamed to admit our struggles to others, or we may fear being judged or rejected. However, as Christians, we are not meant to go through life alone. We are called to be a community of believers who support and encourage one another through life's ups and downs.

In fact, seeking help is a form of faith and trust in God. When we ask for help, we are acknowledging that we cannot do everything on our own and that we need God's grace and the support of others to overcome our challenges. This is a biblical principle that can be seen throughout the Bible.

For example, David and Jonathan's friendship in the Old Testament is an example of two people supporting each other through difficult times. Moses also sought help from Aaron when he struggled to lead the Israelites. Additionally, in the New Testament, Paul encouraged the Galatians to "bear one another's burdens" (Galatians 6:2) and to support each other in love.

Of course, asking for help is not always easy. We may feel ashamed or afraid to admit our struggles to others. However, it is important to remember that seeking help is not a sign of weakness, but rather a brave and wise choice. We can overcome our fears and take practical steps to seek help through prayer, confiding in a trusted friend, or seeking professional counseling.

I first reached for help when I decided that I'd had enough. I was tired of life on the streets and where my crack addiction had taken me. Late one night, I walked through the doors of a drug rehabilitation facility and checked myself in. I was scared and alone. But, I was there. I had come to this decision on my own after almost overdosing earlier that evening. I wanted no more of this life. I was done!

Looking back, I realize that some choices you make along the way to better your life and to fulfill your purpose will require you to make them alone.

The facility I walked into was warm and inviting, but it didn't take away the fear and anxiety I felt inside. At that moment I was determined to take my life back. I was allowed to call my family and let them know I was safe. After the facility checked me in, my reach for help at this point was complete.

Remember, you are not alone in your struggles. God is with you, and there are people who care about you and want to support you through whatever challenges you may be facing. Don't be afraid to reach for help and trust that God will be with you every step of the way.

HUMILITY

Humility is a crucial virtue in the Christian faith. It is the quality of being modest, humble, and respectful of others. The Bible teaches that humility is the key to a healthy relationship with God and with others. James 4:6 states, "God opposes the proud but shows favor to the humble."

Humility involves recognizing that we are not the center of the universe and that we need God's help in our lives. It means acknowledging our limitations, weaknesses, and mistakes. It also means showing respect and kindness to others, regardless of their social status, race, or religion.

Jesus is the perfect example of humility. Although He is the Son of God, He did not consider Himself too important to serve others. He washed the feet of His disciples and willingly suffered on the cross for our sins. Philippians 2:5-8 reads, "In your relationships with one another, have the same mindset as Christ Jesus: Who, being in very nature God, did not consider equality with God something to be used to his own advantage; rather, he made himself nothing by taking the very nature of a servant, being made in human likeness. And being found in appearance as a man, he humbled himself by becoming obedient to death—even death on a cross!"

Humility is not an easy virtue to cultivate. Our culture often values self-promotion, competition, and material success over humility and service. However, as Christians, we are called to a different way of living. We are called to follow Jesus' example of selflessness and love. By practicing humility, we can deepen our relationship with God and become a positive influence in the world around us.

CHANGE

Change is a constant and inevitable part of life. It can be exciting, scary, or difficult, but it always has the potential to bring growth and transformation. As Christians, we believe that God is with us through all seasons of change and that He has a plan for our lives.

As it's been said, change can be a scary thing. It can be uncomfortable and uncertain. However, as Christians, we are called to embrace change and allow God to transform us from the inside out. This transformation can happen in three areas of our lives: our friends, our environment, and our mindset.

Friends

The Bible tells us that "bad company corrupts good character" (1 Corinthians 15:33). It's important to surround ourselves with friends who uplift us, encourage us, and point us toward Christ. If we find ourselves in relationships that are dragging us down or causing us to stumble, we need to pray for the wisdom and courage to make changes. We can trust that God will bring new, positive relationships into our lives.

Environment

Our physical surroundings can have a huge impact on our spiritual and emotional well-being. If we're living in a toxic or unhealthy environment, we need to seek God's guidance on how to make changes. This might mean moving to a new location, decluttering our living space, or making small changes to our daily routine. Whatever the case may be, we can trust that God will guide us toward a place of peace and wholeness.

Mindset

Finally, our mindset is perhaps the most important aspect of change. We need to renew our minds daily with God's truth and allow Him to transform our thoughts and attitudes. This means letting go of negative self-talk, forgiving ourselves and others, and focusing on the things that are true, noble, right, pure, lovely, admirable, excellent, and praiseworthy (Philippians 4:8). When we have a transformed mindset, we'll see the world around us in a new light and be better equipped to handle whatever changes come our way.

Change can be difficult, but it's also necessary for growth and transformation. As Christians, we can trust that God is with us every step of the way, helping us to transform our friends, environment, and mindset for His glory.

My life changed because I changed my mindset, my environment and my friends. I have been completely transformed into the vessel of God's glory that I am today because I had the courage to break off my relationship with my family for a season. Yes! I know that might sound crazy to some of you and it may be a hard decision for some of you to make. But if your spiritual life, growth, and relationship with Christ is important to you, then you won't think twice about what is true.

Separation is good when growth is necessary.

This separation consisted of me limiting the casual time I spent with my family and not attending certain family functions like cookouts, holiday gatherings, birthday celebrations, etc. My biological family was being used by the devil to constantly remind me of my past. They would say mean and evil things like, "you'll be back out there again. You'll want another hit of crack again. It won't be long." The devil used them to taunt me and laugh at me when I praised God out loud. Therefore, I had to separate or, rather, limit my association with them. Notice I said "I" did.

My first priority was my building my relationship with Christ, and I was determined not to let anyone discourage me. I did not want to lose what I had gained and I loved the person I was becoming.

As a result, my life began to soar in every area. My mindset changed and I began to build a stronger relationship with Christ. My faith grew and my understanding of the Word developed. I became empowered with the Holy Spirit. I learned the spiritual discipline of fasting, and in doing so, I heard the voice of God for the first time. I experienced the supernatural realm and saw angels and demons. I even had divine manifestations of Jesus.

One significant occurrence happened at that time. I learned what my purpose was. My calling was made clear. God called me to PREACH.

When you are surrounded by like-minded people, you can't help but prosper.

I joined all the choirs (except the children's choir), which was funny because I felt that I couldn't sing. But my excitement was contagious.

I'd never felt so good in my life! I was soaring! I was in the heavens.

Before I knew it, I had become a prayer intercessor and a Sunday school teacher. Not long after that, the pastor assigned me my own Sunday School class, and I was voted chaplain of one of the choirs.

2 Corinthians 5:17 says, "Therefore, if any man be in Christ, he is a new creature; old things are passed away; behold ALL things are NEW!" God creates new life and gives us everything, including a new identity and a NEW family! I was "becoming" this new person, learning to connect to my "new" church family. It was a beautiful and exciting time in my life.

Moments of Reflection — Application

Did you know...

Transparency is your SUPERPOWER! It is one of the most important steps to SOARING:

BEING HONEST WITH YOURSELF is the essence of Freedom.

In this chapter, you discovered that asking for help is an act of humility and recognition. You cannot handle everything on your own. Humility is a manifestation of faith in God and an acknowledgement of your dependence on Him and others.

Pray and ask the Lord:

- How has what you endured positioned you to be a leader, a mentor, or an example for someone else?

- Why is it important to ask for help?

- Why is it hard for most people to ask for help?

- What was it like for you when you received help?

Notes

CHAPTER TWO

Breaking Free from the Past

We all have a past, but it doesn't have to define us. This chapter will focus on understanding the impact of the past on our present and future and breaking free from sin through repentance, renunciation, and steps to overcoming. Using biblical examples and personal stories of transformation, you will learn how to leave the past behind and move forward with purpose.

It is important to note that healing is not a one-time event, but rather a continuous journey. This section is here to provide you with the tools and support you need to navigate that journey. We understand that this may be a challenging process, and we encourage you to go at your own pace and be kind and compassionate with yourself throughout the process.

UNDERSTANDING THE CAGE

Have you ever felt trapped in a cycle of sin? Maybe it started small, with a small compromise here or a little lie there. But before you knew it, the sin had taken hold and you found yourself unable to break free.

When we find ourselves trapped in sin, it can feel like we're stuck in a cage. No matter how hard we try, we can't seem to break free from the sin that has ensnared us. But understanding the nature of this cage can be the first step in finding freedom.

The cage of sin is made up of lies and deception. It tells us that the sin we're engaging in is harmless, that it's not hurting anyone, that we can stop anytime we want to. But these are all lies that keep us trapped in the cycle of sin.

The cage of sin also isolates us from the support and accountability we need to break free. We may feel ashamed or embarrassed to admit our struggles to others, or we may be afraid of being judged or rejected. But it's only when we bring our struggles into the light that we can find the help and support we need to overcome.

Finally, the cage of sin keeps us focused on ourselves and our own desires, rather than on God and His plan for our lives. We may feel like we're in control, but in reality, we're being controlled by our sin. Only when we surrender our desires and our will to God can we find true freedom.

If you're feeling trapped in a cycle of sin, know that you're not alone. There is hope and there is a way out of the cage. By understanding the nature of the cage of sin and seeking help and support from others, we can break free and experience the abundant life that God has for us.

How Sins Affect Our Lives

Sin is a powerful force that can have a devastating impact on our lives. It promises pleasure and fulfillment, but in reality, it only leads to captivity and destruction. While we often think of sin in terms of its moral implications, the truth is that it can have tangible consequences as well.

When we sin, we open ourselves up to a variety of negative consequences. For example, if we engage in addictive behaviors such as substance abuse or pornography, we may find that these behaviors begin to dominate our lives. We may lose control over our actions and find it difficult to break free from these destructive patterns.

Sin can also have an impact on our mental and emotional well-being. We may experience feelings of guilt, shame, and remorse as a result of our actions, which can lead to depression and anxiety. We may also find that our relationships with others are damaged as a result of our sin.

But perhaps the greatest cost of captivity is the damage it does to our relationship with God. When we sin, we turn away from God and become separated from Him. This separation can lead to feelings of loneliness, despair, and hopelessness.

Despite the cost of captivity, there is hope. Through Christ, we can find forgiveness and freedom from the chains of sin. By acknowledging our sin and turning to God, we can experience the healing and restoration that only He can provide.

However, sin affects our lives in ways that may not always be immediately apparent.

Sin separates us from God. When we choose to follow our own desires and ignore God's commands, we distance ourselves from Him. As a result, we lose the joy and peace that come with a close relationship with God.

Sin creates chains that keep us bound. It may start with a small habit or a seemingly harmless decision, but sin can quickly become a stronghold that controls our thoughts, emotions, and actions. These chains of captivity can be difficult to break, but with God's help, we can find freedom.

Sin damages our relationships with others. The selfishness and pride that come with sin often lead to hurt and brokenness in our relationships with family, friends, and even strangers. The consequences of sin ripple outward and affect those around us.

Sin has a cost that we cannot pay. The Bible teaches that the wages of sin is death (Romans 6:23). We are all deserving of death and eternal separation from God because of our sin, but God provided a way for us to be reconciled to Him through Jesus Christ.

Repentance and Renunciation

Repentance and renunciation are two key aspects of the Christian faith that are often intertwined. Repentance involves acknowledging and confessing our sins before God, while renunciation involves turning away from those sins and actively seeking to live a life that honors God.

In the Bible, we see numerous examples of repentance and renunciation. King David, for instance, wrote Psalm 51 after he was confronted with his sin of adultery and murder. In the psalm, he cries out to God, confesses his wrongdoing, and asks for forgiveness. Similarly, the Apostle Paul had a powerful encounter with God that led him to turn away from his former ways and become a devoted follower of Jesus.

Repentance and renunciation require humility and a willingness to admit our faults and shortcomings. It can be painful to confront our sin and turn away from it, but it is necessary for spiritual growth and transformation. As Christians, we are called to live lives that are set apart and holy, and repentance and renunciation are essential in this process.

In order to practice repentance and renunciation, we must first recognize areas of our lives where we are not aligned with God's will. This could be anything from harboring bitterness and unforgiveness toward someone to engaging in behaviors that are harmful to ourselves or others. We must then confess these sins to God and ask for forgiveness, trusting in His mercy and grace to cleanse us.

Renunciation involves taking active steps to turn away from our sinful behaviors and attitudes. This may involve seeking accountability from a trusted friend or mentor, setting boundaries to protect ourselves from temptation, and seeking God's help and strength to resist temptation and make positive changes in our lives.

Repentance and renunciation are essential practices for Christians who desire to live lives that honor God. By confessing our sins and turning away from them, we open ourselves up to the transformative power of God's love and grace. May we all strive to practice repentance and renunciation in our daily lives, and may God help us to grow in holiness and spiritual maturity.

STEPS TO OVERCOMING SINS

Overcoming sins means recognizing and acknowledging our own sinful nature and actively working toward living a life that is pleasing to God. The Bible teaches that all human beings are sinners and fall short of the glory of God (Romans 3:23). However, as Christians, we are called to resist and overcome sin through the power of the Holy Spirit.

Overcoming sin does not mean that we will never sin again or that we will become perfect in this life. It means that we recognize our weaknesses and are committed to making positive changes in our lives to honor God. It means that we confess our sins, repent, and seek God's forgiveness and guidance.

As we strive to overcome sin, we can draw on the strength and wisdom of God through prayer, Scripture, and the support of our Christian community. Overcoming sin is a lifelong process that requires humility, perseverance, and faith. It is a journey toward becoming more like Christ and living a life that reflects His love and grace to the world.

Overcoming sin is an important aspect of the Christian life, but it can also be a difficult and ongoing struggle. Here are some practical steps to help you overcome sin and live a life that honors God:

Confess your sin: Confession is the first step toward overcoming sin. Admitting your wrongs and seeking forgiveness from God and those you have wronged can bring healing and restoration.

Repent: Repentance means turning away from sin and turning toward God. Ask the Holy Spirit to help you identify the root causes of your sin and make a conscious effort to turn away from those behaviors and attitudes.

Renew your mind: Romans 12:2 encourages us to renew our minds and be transformed by the renewing of our minds. This means replacing negative and sinful thoughts with positive and godly ones. Meditate on Scripture and surround yourself with positive influences that will encourage and strengthen you in your faith.

Seek accountability: Having an accountability partner or community can help you stay on track and provide encouragement and support. Find someone you trust who can hold you accountable and check in with you regularly.

Pray: Prayer is a powerful tool for overcoming sin. Ask God to give you the strength and courage to resist temptation and stay on the path toward righteousness.

Remember, overcoming sin is not a one-time event, but a daily process. Keep pressing forward and trust in God's grace and guidance as you strive toward a life that honors Him.

UNDERSTANDING THE IMPACT OF THE PAST ON OUR PRESENT AND FUTURE

As Christians, we believe that our past experiences, both good and bad, have a significant impact on our present and future. The Bible teaches us that we are shaped by our experiences, and that we are called to seek healing and wholeness in every area of our lives.

However, sometimes the wounds of our past can be difficult to overcome. We may find ourselves struggling with negative thought patterns, unhealthy relationships, or destructive habits that are rooted in past experiences. Without understanding the impact of our past on our present and future, we may find ourselves stuck in a cycle of pain and dysfunction.

Even as believers, we have to face the harsh reality that healing is work. There is not a one-time antidote for it. Healing takes time. The deeper the wound, the longer it takes to heal.

Emotional scars can take a lifetime to heal. They tend to reappear when we least expect it. Even as believers, we still have issues we wrestle with from our past. Not all of our "demons" are destroyed or our illnesses healed just because we in a relationship with Christ.

A couple of times, early in my pastorate, I had a mental breakdown and sunk into a deep depression. Dealing with the death of a family member or a congregant would trigger feelings and thoughts, which would resort in a desire to use drugs. Voices from my past days of addiction, the sensory memory of taste and smell would manifest. Using drugs as a temporary form of escape was what I did then.

But I've learned to seek strength and help in my community of believers, in the word of God, and on my knees in the presence of God. I thank God for the growth and maturity in my life. Because of the work that I put in, I've been able to maintain my freedom and new life in Him.

As followers of Christ, we have hope. Through prayer, counseling, and support from our Christian community, we can begin to understand the impact of our past experiences and find healing and restoration. By acknowledging and addressing the wounds of our past, we can begin to break free from the negative patterns that have held us back and move forward into the abundant life that God has for us. With God's help, we can find healing and wholeness in every area of our lives and step into the fullness of the abundant life that He has for us.

BIBLICAL EXAMPLES OF BREAKING FREE FROM THE PAST

As Christians, we are called to leave our old lives behind and walk in newness of life with Christ (Romans 6:4). It can be challenging to break free from the past and the patterns of behavior and thoughts that may have held us captive for years.

Thankfully, the Bible is filled with examples of individuals who overcame their past and walked in freedom with God. One such example is Paul, who was once a persecutor of Christians but later became a faithful servant of Christ. In Philippians 3:13-14, Paul writes, "But one thing I do: forgetting what lies behind and straining forward to what lies ahead, I press on toward the goal for the prize of the upward call of God in Christ Jesus."

Another example is Joseph, who was sold into slavery by his own brothers but later rose to become a powerful leader in Egypt. Despite the hardships he faced, Joseph chose to forgive his brothers and trust in God's plan for his life. As he tells his brothers in Genesis 50:20, "As for you, you meant evil against me, but God meant it for good, to bring it about that many people should be kept alive, as they are today."

These stories, along with many others in the Bible, demonstrate that with God's help, it is possible to break free from the past and walk in freedom and wholeness. As we look to these examples, let us be encouraged to press on toward the goal and trust in God's plan for our lives, even when it seems difficult or uncertain. With His help, we can leave our past behind and walk confidently into the future He has prepared for us.

Moments of Reflection — Application

Now that you have studied how the past impacts our lives:

What negative traits do you see operating in your life today?

Remember healing is not a one-time event, it's a continuous journey. You have to go at it at your own pace and be patient with yourself throughout the process.

Seek God in your private moments of meditation and prayer for guidance and direction. Ask Him to reveal what's hidden inside of you that may be lingering and listen intentionally for His response.

Notes

CHAPTER THREE

Finally, I Know Who I Am

In a world full of distractions and competing voices, it's easy to lose sight of who we truly are. We may define ourselves by our career, our relationships, or our possessions, but these external factors can be unstable and fleeting. As Christians, however, we have the opportunity to ground our identity in something deeper and more enduring, our relationship with Christ.

In this chapter, we will explore what it means to find our identity in Christ. Through Scripture, personal stories, and practical insights, we will discover the freedom and purpose that come from embracing who God created us to be. Whether you are struggling with self-doubt, searching for direction, or simply wanting to grow closer to Jesus, this book offers a roadmap for finding your identity in Him.

Our identity is not defined by our past, our circumstances, or even our own accomplishments. It is rooted in our relationship with Christ. This chapter will explore the importance of surrendering to Christ and letting go of control, as well as personal accounts of Christ's transforming power. By understanding our identity in Christ, we can live with confidence and purpose.

BROKEN

My mom and dad's marriage was coming to an end when I was conceived. So, I wasn't welcomed nor wanted by either of them. But I had a divine purpose for God.

I was hidden in my mother's womb, by her menstrual cycle, for six months before she found out she was pregnant with me. And even when she did find out, she wanted a boy and she was disappointed that I was a girl.

I grew up in a home filled with partying. On one of those usual "party nights" for Mama, my brother and I were unsupervised, left alone once again.

It was a hot summer night. No school. We were sitting on the front porch with mostly his friends. I was considered a tomboy. My brother and I are only a year apart, so his friends were my friends.

Earlier that day, I had played a rough game of football with the fellas and we were happily hanging out on the porch until nightfall. I decided to go to bed and left the crowd. My brother had the record player playing on full volume.

I jumped in the shower and put on this beautiful powder blue and white chiffon gown that my older sister had given me. I cherished that gown. That night was my first time wearing it.

We had a bottom floor apartment with no air conditioning. I was dozing off when suddenly a hand covered my mouth and a voice told me to be quiet. At the same time, he was tearing at my clothes.

I was only twelve years old, and just like that, my virginity was gone. I couldn't believe I had been raped. Although it was quick, it seemed like a lifetime. Passionless and painful, fueled by his desire to have me and his anxiety to not get caught by my brother, he was in a rush. Hate filled my heart when it was over.

I conceived a child as a result of the rape. I became bitter and suicidal and angry. Guilt and shame filled me as well. I felt as if I placed a dark cloud over my family.

BOUND

Not only had I conceived as a result of that traumatic event, I was just a child myself. The news rocked not only me, but also my family, neighbors, and community. The public shame had a suffocating hold on me. The guilt I carried, believing that I had brought shame upon my family, was almost unbearable for me as a child. It was one thing to feel the shame that came with being a victim of rape, but it was another thing entirely to face the additional shame and stigma that came with being pregnant as a result.

At such a young age, I was subjected to a multitude of traumas that no child should ever have to face. The stress, whispers, lies, gossip, and name-calling all became a part of my daily life.

The shame and isolation that I felt was overwhelming. As a child, I didn't understand the adult conversations about abortion and adoption that my mother and her friends were having. They spoke in hushed tones and sent me to my bedroom, alone with my thoughts and the sensation of something moving inside of me. The weight of it all was too much to bear, and I found myself feeling increasingly isolated and broken.

Suicidal thoughts began to visit me more frequently. I blamed myself for the shame my family endured, and I felt that I was the one who had brought this darkness upon us. In my mind, I believed I should have fought harder or yelled louder. But nobody took the time to sit me down and explain what had happened, comfort me, or assure me that everything was going to be alright.

My mother's sisters and friends were quick to offer their opinions and ask if she was okay, but I was the one carrying the baby. It was as if my feelings and well-being were not even a consideration. The scandal of my pregnancy spread through the neighborhood like wildfire, and my family was left to bear the weight of the shame that I had brought upon them.

In the end, I was left feeling completely alone and abandoned. No one took the time to understand what I was going through or offer me the support I so desperately needed.

During this difficult period, my stepfather subjected me to torment by disbelieving my account of being assaulted. Instead, he labeled me as "fast" or "easy" (terms used at the time). He would use any opportunity to taunt me with these words. At that time, we both harbored strong animosity toward each other. My hatred toward him stemmed from two reasons: he was an alcoholic and regularly beat my mother, my brother, and me when he was drunk, and he whipped me with a belt when I was eight months pregnant. I felt lost and in pain with no one to turn to. Guilt, shame, pain, and emptiness were all bottled up inside me.

Once a bubbly young girl, I became a prisoner of my own thoughts, losing my voice and the ability to speak up for myself. I was bound.

JESUS THE RESCUER: OUR SAVIOR AND REDEEMER

Have you ever found yourself in a difficult situation like me, feeling trapped and helpless? Maybe you've made mistakes, or bad decisions, or perhaps circumstances outside of your control have left you feeling lost and alone. Whatever the reason, we've all experienced moments where we've needed rescuing. The good news is there is someone who can help us. His name is Jesus, and He is our Savior and Redeemer.

Before we can fully appreciate the rescuing power of Jesus, we must understand why we need rescuing in the first place. The Bible tells us that all have sinned and fall short of the glory of God (Romans 3:23). In other words, we've all made mistakes and done things that go against God's perfect standards. These mistakes create a separation between us and God, and we are unable to bridge that gap on our own.

Thankfully, God didn't leave us to fend for ourselves. He sent his son Jesus to rescue us from our sin and reconcile us to Himself. Jesus lived a perfect life, died on the cross for our sins, and rose from the dead on the third day. Through His sacrifice, He paid the penalty for our sins and made a way for us to be forgiven and reconciled to God.

Our response to Jesus, knowing that He has the power to rescue us, is only the first step. We must also respond to Him in faith and accept the gift of salvation He offers us. This means acknowledging our need for rescue, confessing our sins, and putting our trust in Jesus as our Savior and Lord.

When we put our faith in Jesus, we become new creations. The old has passed away, and the new has come (2 Corinthians 5:17). We are no longer defined by our past mistakes and failures but are instead redeemed and transformed by the love of Christ. This redemption is not just for our own benefit but also allows us to become agents of change in the world, sharing the love and rescuing power of Jesus with others.

In a world that can often feel dark and hopeless, it is comforting to know that we have a Rescuer who loves us and has the power to save us. Jesus is our Savior and Redeemer, and when we put our trust in Him, we can experience the fullness of His love and grace. So if you find yourself in need of rescue, turn to Jesus and let Him be your Rescuer too.

Christ's Transforming Power

Ten years later, I was at a point in my life where I had become a hopeless crack addict. I was also a prostitute, and boy, do I have stories to tell. Living a life of homelessness on the streets, I was a complete and utter mess.

I was chained to a life of darkness and despair. I had crawled into a cesspool with murderers, pimps, gangbangers, con men, ex-cons, prostitutes, homosexuals and thieves. You name them, they were there, and I was among them and was one of them.

How did I get there? How did I land in the devil's den as one of his slaves? Chained to an addiction that drug me into places I would drive my car through, let alone sit and get high in.

"Pull up a chair. Have a seat," she said. There was a stench of crack smoke and unbathed bodies in the air. The chair she offered me to sit in and the couches and chairs that were around were stained, old and beat up, covered in God knows what. It was like walking into a cold morgue. Last week's heroin and crack addicts looked like zombies slumped over, sleeping or dazed (geeked), and there were heroin addicts with needles sticking out of their arms.

The paint on the walls was chipped and peeling. A cold damp feeling permeated the air as I walked in. Looking back, it's quite indescribable and sad. There were no pictures on the wall, no décor on the tables, no family photos in picture frames, just a rickety TV stand with a faulty television playing and dingy curtains hanging off a broken curtain rod on the window. There was nothing warm or inviting about the place. It was just what it was...the devil's den.

As long as you had a crack rock to smoke, or money to buy one, you were welcome to relax, drink, or eat (if you could) in the crack house. But be sure to pay the house in crack, sex, or cash (sometimes both). If the dealer wanted you, you would pay with sex and cash. Then you were free to smoke away.

But, when it was all over, OH! the shame, guilt, pain and regret. Thoughts of death became sweeter and more appealing. Inside, all I really wanted was my momma. I wanted to be held. I would scream for her, long for her and wanted to be home.

THE DAY I MET JESUS

After another dark week of surviving in the concrete jungle, another tormenting cycle of emptiness, shame and pain came to an end.

I was broke, hopeless, ashamed, scared and alone. I wanted to go home, but this time, I pulled someone else into my ugly world: my live-in boyfriend.

For this rendezvous, I stole his car. Really wanting to be free, I tried to return to a life of normalcy around this time of my addiction. I met my boyfriend, and because he wasn't a user, I thought somehow he would be my way out of the darkness.

For a short time, it seemed as if it worked. We moved in together, I got a job and all was well. Until one day, the demons rose up within me wanting a taste.

That's one of the worst feelings you can ever have: thinking you have conquered a thing only to find out it's still there.

A new way of living doesn't destroy a devil. Only the power of God can. "If any man be in Christ, he is a new man; old things have passed away; behold, all things have become new" (2 Corinthians 5:17).

I went to work that Monday and returned home that Saturday afternoon. I felt like the prodigal son. I went to my sister's apartment. I had made up my mind that I was done with living. It was time to end the vicious cycle. I couldn't take it anymore. I didn't want to go on living like this or taking my family through this. So, I decided that day would be the day. But first, I wanted to see my newborn nephew.

So, I went to my sister's house. My family greeted me, not with words of relief but anger. "Where have you been? ... You could've called. ... Why do you keep doing this? ... You know you lost your job? ... Have you taken a bath?" All kinds of questions with knives in every word.

But Momma asked, "Have you eaten?" ... Are you ok? ...Are you tired? ... Are you hurt anywhere?"

I didn't know what to say. I had no words. I just wanted a hug from anyone...someone...but I only had Momma's words.

I just wanted to see the baby but so much was being hurled at me. I was in a whirlwind. Insults and anger were being thrown at me all at once and I wanted to get out.

Someone called my boyfriend and told him I had come back. He showed up yelling louder and louder. My sister was in tears, screaming. Momma tried to quiet everyone down and I was sitting there feeling dirty, dejected, rejected, and unwanted with my face hidden in my hand, bawling. The only voice that was louder than any of theirs was the one in my ear telling me, "Just get it over with! Just kill yourself, you'll be better off! You'll show 'em!"

After they all said what they needed to say, I somehow found myself alone in the living room. I went into the kitchen and opened the utensil drawer and got the butcher's knife. I quietly sneaked into the bathroom and locked the door. I shut off the lights. I remember trembling, my heart was racing, and I was terrified. Not because of what I was getting ready to do. I didn't want to get caught, and I wanted death to be quick and painless. I didn't want it to hurt.

So, with the lights off and my back against the wall, I faced the toilet and gripped the handle of the knife tightly pressing it into my chest underneath my breast. I closed my eyes and began to pray. At the time, I didn't realize that's what I was doing. But I turned my face upwards with my eyes closed and said, "Lord, forgive me. I can't take it anymore."

The next thing I remember, a bright light opened above me...a portal. A silhouette of a man appeared above me (I now know it was Jesus) and His hand reached down through the portal and grabbed my hand and the knife and pulled me off of the floor. I was speechless. I couldn't believe my eyes. It happened so fast, and just like that, the portal closed and the knife fell on the floor and my boyfriend opened the door and cut on the lights. I was dazed from what happened and couldn't speak. He and my sister were yelling and screaming. Looking back at that moment, I tried to figure out how he got in the bathroom. I know I locked the door. It couldn't have been anyone else but Jesus that let him in.

This was the day I met Jesus. I knew from that day forward my life would be changed forever.

I was given instructions by the Lord to go to church on that Sunday, and I obeyed. That day the Lord touched my heart. I heard from God, and since then my life has changed forever.

SURRENDERING TO CHRIST: LETTING GO OF CONTROL

Surrendering to Christ is not an easy task, especially when we are used to being in control of our lives. But letting go of control and trusting in Christ is essential for our spiritual growth and well-being.

Surrendering to Christ is the act of giving up control of our lives and submitting to His will. It means acknowledging that God's plan for our lives is greater than our own and trusting that He will guide us in the right direction. Surrendering to Christ requires humility, trust, and a willingness to let go of our own desires and plans.

Surrendering to anyone is not an easy thing to do, and let's be honest, that includes God too. God keeps so much of what He has in store for us a mystery: the way He's going to take us, who's involved in getting us where He's taking us, what we'll need to get there, and so on. Sometimes, it can feel like there are so many missing pieces to the puzzle, and that can scare you.

Two main elements made it easy for me to surrender to the Lord: my pure LOVE for Him and my absolute TRUST in Him. These two feelings of adoration for the Lord Jesus Christ made giving Him control over my life and obeying His commands easy.

After I got saved, I planned on living what I thought would be a normal married life, work at the bank and serve in the auxiliaries at the church. I was content with where things were going in my life. Not long after things settled down in my life, my boyfriend and I were married. And I had moved to a higher paying job at the Federal Reserve Bank and was offered a side job in modeling. Things were looking up.

My Sunday school class was growing and life was on another level. Not to mention, I was able to attend family gatherings again without ridicule. My family saw that I wasn't the old person I used to be. My life had changed completely. I was transformed. They knew I had been born again. That I had really been delivered.

They grew to respect me. Several were coming to me for prayer. Some of my family members had given their lives to Christ as a result of seeing how my life had transformed under His control and my submission, love, trust and obedience to Him. My mom and sister joined the church I attended.

One Wednesday night, my pastor had finished preaching. He came down from the pulpit and stood in front of the congregation. He said there were ten people in the sanctuary that the Lord had called to preach. As the Spirit led, he began pointing at certain people in the congregation to identify who some of them were. He told a few of them to come forward so he could pray for them. I was not one of them.

I was seated next to my boyfriend. I heard a voice as if he had spoken the words to me, "You're one of them." I turned my head quickly and looked at my husband. I asked, "Did you say something?" He said no, and no one was seated to my right. But I had heard the words in my right ear. Seconds later, I heard the same words again. I didn't say anything more to my husband, I just sat there in amazement. I sensed the warmth of a Presence upon me.

When we left the service, I was in a trance. And that night, going forward, I began to have visions and dreams of myself in front of people from different angles and from different views.

I would be on the platform in what appeared to be stadiums. Or, I would be standing in pulpits at the podium. I'd be laying hands on people, and they would fall out under the power of God. He was pretty much showing me doing things my pastor was doing.

I had one experience where God took me to hell. I saw lost souls being tortured and burned. They were crying out, screaming in agony. It was horrible. Some of the souls were in caves, chained to walls and they were being tortured by demons with pitchforks.

I woke up in my room, shaking, in tears. I thought it was a bad dream. A sense of relief rushed over me. And as I was about to shrug it off, the Lord suddenly burst through with His voice and called my name. "Teky!" He said. "What you just saw are the souls of the people that YOU lost because you didn't accept your calling." I was horrified. I cried.

I was taken to hell because I had told the Lord that I didn't want to preach. After that, I surrendered. Thirty years later, I can proudly say I have no regrets.

When you come from a place of darkness, chaos and confusion, and you've been brought to a place of light and love, you have a different perspective of what handing over control of your life to the Lord means.

You're made to feel that you are worth more than anything on earth. Because to God, you are. I know that my steps are ordered by the

Lord and that His plans are unfolding in my life. If I obey and follow His lead, I will be ok.

He says in His word, "All things work together for good, to them that love the Lord and to those who are called according to His purpose."

Trusting the Lord's purpose for our lives allows us to experience true freedom and peace. When we try to control every aspect of our lives, we often end up feeling stressed, anxious, and overwhelmed. But when we surrender to Christ, we can trust that He has our best interests at heart and that He will take care of us. Surrendering to Christ also helps us to develop a closer relationship with God and to become more like Him.

Surrendering to Christ is a daily process that requires intentional effort. Here are some ways we can surrender to Christ:

- Spend time in prayer and bible study to align our hearts and minds with God's will.

- Choose to trust God even when things don't make sense.

- Give thanks in all circumstances, knowing that God is in control.

- Seek wise counsel and accountability from other believers.

- Surrender our fears, doubts, and worries to God and ask Him to take control.

Remember surrendering to Christ is not a one-time event but a daily practice. It requires us to let go of our desire for control and to trust in God's plan for our lives. As we surrender to Christ, we will experience the peace and freedom that only He can provide. May we all strive to surrender our lives to Him and to trust in His unfailing love and grace.

Importance of Understanding our Identity in Christ

Our identity in Christ is not based on what we do, what we have, or what others think of us. It is rooted in who we are in Him. When we accept Jesus Christ as our Savior, we become children of God and heirs to His kingdom. Our identity is now found in Him, not in the things of this world.

Understanding our identity in Christ is crucial because it shapes the way we see ourselves and the world around us. When we know who we are in Him, we have a sense of purpose and direction. We're not defined by our past mistakes, our current circumstances, or our future uncertainties. Instead, we're secure in our identity as children of God, and that gives us confidence and hope.

Knowing our identity in Christ can transform every aspect of our lives. It can change the way we think, act, and relate to others. When we realize that we are loved, accepted, and forgiven by God, we're free to be ourselves and to pursue our God-given purposes. We no longer have to seek validation from others or from the things of this world. We're empowered by the Holy Spirit to live a life of meaning and impact.

Your identity in Christ is the key to a fulfilling life. By understanding who you are in Him, you can experience the joy, peace, and purpose that come from living in relationship with God.

Moments of Reflection—Application

Take a moment and listen on purpose to the Voice.

Surrendering to Christ is the act of letting go and it is not an easy thing to do. It means that you will have to give up complete control of your life and submit to His will.

You will need to ask the Holy Spirit in prayer to help you surrender to the will of Christ and let go of your own desires and plans.

- *What are some specific areas in your life that are difficult for you to let go?

- What are your strongest desires and why are they hard for you to surrender to Christ?

- Have you discovered your identity in Christ?

- How has your life been since your discovery?

- How has it affected others in your life?

- How has it affected you?

- Finding your purpose in Christ: Where is the FIRE burning within you to serve/help?

Notes

CHAPTER FOUR

THE POWER OF FORGIVENESS

Forgiveness is a concept that is deeply rooted in the Christian faith. It is the act of releasing someone from the debt of wrongdoing. Forgiveness can be difficult, and yet it is an essential component of a healthy and peaceful life. In this chapter, we will talk about the power of forgiveness and how it can transform our lives. We will learn how forgiveness can heal wounds, restore relationships, and bring us closer to God. Through real-life stories and practical advice, we will discover how forgiveness can be a catalyst for personal growth and spiritual renewal.

Forgiveness is a key to freedom and soaring. It is the hard part of letting go of past hurts, forgiving those who have hurt us, and even forgiving ourselves. This chapter will explore the importance of forgiveness in the journey to freedom and purpose, as well as practical tips for how to forgive and let go of past hurts. Using biblical examples and personal stories of forgiveness, we will learn how to build a strong foundation for deepening our relationship with God.

FORGIVENESS

Forgiveness is the act of pardoning someone for wrongdoing. It involves letting go of resentment and anger toward the offender. Forgiveness is not forgetting the offense, but it is choosing to release the offender from the debt they owe us.

Forgiveness is an essential part of the Christian faith. We are called to forgive those who have hurt us, just as God has forgiven us. However, forgiveness can be difficult, especially when we have been deeply hurt by someone. It can be even harder to forgive ourselves when we have made mistakes and hurt others.

But forgiveness is not just a suggestion, it is a commandment from God. In Matthew 6:14-15, Jesus says, "For if you forgive other people when they sin against you, your heavenly Father will also forgive you. But if you do not forgive others their sins, your father will not forgive your sins." This shows us that forgiveness is not optional for Christians.

Forgiveness does not mean that we forget what has happened or that we condone the behavior of the person who hurt us. It simply means that we release the anger and bitterness we feel toward them and choose to move forward with love and compassion.

Forgiving ourselves can be just as challenging as forgiving others. It is easy to get caught up in guilt and shame for our past mistakes, but God calls us to let go of our self-condemnation and accept His forgiveness. In 1 John 1:9, we are told, "If we confess our sins, he is faithful and just and will forgive us our sins and purify us from all unrighteousness."

When we forgive ourselves, we are not excusing our actions, but rather acknowledging that we are human and capable of making mistakes. We can learn from our past mistakes and use them to grow in our faith and become better people.

Forgiveness is an important part of the Christian faith. It may be difficult, but it is necessary for our own spiritual growth and well-being. When we forgive those who have hurt us and ourselves, we are able to move forward in life with a sense of freedom and peace.

LIVING A LIFE OF FREEDOM AND PURPOSE

As Christians, we believe that our purpose in life is to glorify God and enjoy Him forever. However, in a world full of distractions, temptations, and trials, it can be difficult to stay focused on our purpose and experience the freedom that Christ offers us. We believe that Jesus Christ died on the cross to set us free from sin and death.

Through His sacrifice, we have been given a new life, a life of freedom and purpose. But what does it mean to live a life of freedom and purpose? And how can we live this out in our everyday lives?

The Bible tells us that "if the Son sets you free, you will be free indeed" (John 8:36). But what does it mean to be free in Christ? It means that we are no longer slaves to sin, fear, or the expectations of others. We have been forgiven of our sins and have been given a new identity as children of God. This freedom allows us to live our lives with confidence, knowing that we are loved and accepted by our heavenly Father.

The first step to living a life of freedom and purpose is to understand what freedom really means. As Christians, we know that true freedom isn't just the absence of constraints or limitations, but it's the ability to live in accordance with God's will for our lives. When we're free, we're able to live the life that God has called us to live, without being held back by sin or fear. But this kind of freedom isn't something that we can achieve on our own – it's a gift that's given to us through faith in Jesus Christ.

Once we understand what it means to be free, we can start to discover our purpose in life. God has a unique plan for each one of us, and when we're living in accordance with that plan, we experience a sense of fulfillment and joy that can't be found anywhere else. But how do we find our purpose? The first step is to seek God's will for our lives through prayer and studying His word. As we spend time in God's presence, we'll begin to understand the gifts and talents that He's given us, and we'll be able to use those gifts to serve others and bring glory to God.

Living a life of freedom and purpose is all about putting what we've learned into practice. This means making choices that are in line with God's will for our lives, even when it's difficult or unpopular. It means serving others with the gifts and talents that God has given us and using those gifts to make a positive impact in the world. And it means seeking God's guidance and direction in everything that we do, so that we can stay on the path that He has set before us.

Living a life of freedom and purpose is a journey, and it's not always easy. But when we trust in God and follow His lead, we can experience a sense of fulfillment and joy that can't be found anywhere else. So let's embrace the freedom that Christ has given us, and let's live our lives with purpose, knowing that we're making a difference in the world and bringing glory to God.

Importance of Forgiveness in the Journey to Freedom and Soaring

Forgiveness is vital for our emotional, spiritual, and physical well-being. Unforgiveness can lead to bitterness, resentment, and anger, which can harm our relationships with others and with God.

Forgiveness allows us to let go of negative emotions and move on from the offense.

Forgiveness is an essential part of the journey to freedom and soaring. When we hold on to unforgiveness, we are weighed down by the burden of anger and bitterness. But when we choose to forgive, we are set free from the emotional baggage that we carry. Forgiveness allows us to soar above our circumstances and reach new heights in our faith.

Forgiveness is not always easy, but it is possible. We can start by praying for the person who hurt us and asking God for the strength to forgive them. We can also seek counsel from a pastor or Christian counselor who can guide us through the process of forgiveness. As we practice forgiveness, we will experience the freedom and soaring that comes with it.

Forgiveness is essential for our journey as Christians. It allows us to let go of negative emotions and move on from the offenses we have experienced. As we practice forgiveness, we will experience the freedom and soaring that comes with it. Let us choose to forgive as God forgives us, and may we soar to new heights in our faith.

Forgiveness Is An Important Step For Deliverance

Forgiveness is an important step in the process of deliverance because it allows individuals to let go of negative emotions and resentments that can hold them back from healing and moving forward in their lives. When we hold on to hurt and anger, it can consume our thoughts and emotions, creating a cycle of pain and resentment. This can lead to feelings of depression, anxiety, and even physical health issues.

Forgiveness allows individuals to break this cycle by releasing the negative emotions and resentments they are holding on to. It can also help to improve relationships, reduce stress and tension, and promote feelings of peace and well-being.

Additionally, forgiveness can also be an important step in the spiritual aspect of deliverance. Many religious and spiritual traditions view forgiveness as a fundamental aspect of personal growth and spiritual development. It is often seen as a way to release negative energy and emotions and allow for a deeper connection to one's faith and spirituality.

Forgiveness is an important step in deliverance because it allows individuals to release things that can hold them back from healing and move forward in their lives, and it can also be a spiritual aspect to connect with oneself and one's faith.

BUILDING A STRONG FOUNDATION

When you think of building a house, what is the first thing that comes to mind? Perhaps you picture laying a sturdy foundation of concrete and rebar, one that can withstand the weight of the entire structure. Without a solid foundation, a building is vulnerable to collapse, unable to weather the storms that inevitably come. In the same way, our spiritual lives require a strong foundation if they are to endure the challenges of this world.

Building a strong foundation is a concept that resonates with Christians. Jesus talks about the importance of a strong foundation in Matthew 7:24-27. In this passage, He says, "Therefore everyone who hears these words of mine and puts them into practice is like a wise man who built his house on the rock. The rain came down, the streams rose, and the winds blew and beat against that house; yet it did not fall, because it had its foundation on the rock. But everyone who hears these words of mine and does not put them into practice is like a foolish man who built his house on sand. The rain came down, the streams rose, and the winds blew and beat against that house, and it fell with a great crash."

To build a strong foundation, we must first understand what makes up a strong foundation. A strong spiritual foundation consists of four key components: faith, prayer, bible study, and community. Each of these components is interrelated and essential to building a strong foundation that can withstand life's challenges.

FAITH

Faith is the cornerstone of building a strong foundation. Hebrews 11:6 tells us that "without faith it is impossible to please God." Faith is the foundation upon which our relationship with God is built, and it is the means by which we receive the promises of God. Faith enables us to trust God even when we cannot see the outcome. To build our faith, we must cultivate it through prayer, worship, and studying God's Word.

PRAYER

Prayer is the means by which we communicate with God. Prayer enables us to align our hearts with God's will and to seek His guidance and wisdom. James 5:16 tells us that "the prayer of a righteous person is powerful and effective." When we pray, we are acknowledging our dependence on God and our need for His help. Prayer is essential to building a strong foundation because it strengthens our relationship with God and deepens our faith.

Bible Study

The Bible is the Word of God, and it is the foundation upon which our faith is built. Bible study enables us to gain a deeper understanding of God's Word and to apply it to our lives. Psalm 119:105 tells us that "Your word is a lamp to my feet and a light to my path." When we study the Bible, we are equipping ourselves with the knowledge and wisdom we need to navigate life's challenges. Bible study is essential to building a strong foundation because it enables us to know God and to grow in our faith.

Community

God designed us for community. We were not meant to live in isolation, but rather to live in community with one another. Proverbs 27:17 tells us that "As iron sharpens iron, so one person sharpens another." We need other believers to encourage us, support us, and hold us accountable. Community is essential to building a strong foundation because it provides us with a sense of belonging and support.

Building a strong foundation is not a one-time event; it is a lifelong process. We must be intentional about maintaining our foundation by avoiding common pitfalls such as doubt, sin, and lack of discipline. James 1:6-8 tells us that "the one who doubts is like a wave of the sea, blown and tossed by the wind." We must guard our hearts against doubt and seek God's wisdom and guidance. We must also guard against sin and be disciplined in our pursuit of righteousness.

Building a strong foundation is essential to living a fulfilling and purposeful life. As we cultivate our faith, pray, study the Bible, and engage in community, we are building a foundation that can withstand life's challenges. We can build a foundation that will stand the test of time and enable us to live the life that He has called us to.

Tips for Deepening Our Relationship with God

As Christians, we are called to have a deep and intimate relationship with God. This relationship is not only vital to our spiritual growth but also to our well-being. However, many of us struggle to connect with God on a personal level. We often get so caught up in our daily routines that we forget to spend time with Him. These are some practical ways that can help us draw closer to God.

Prayer

Prayer is an essential tool for deepening our relationship with God. It allows us to communicate with Him, express our gratitude, and seek guidance.

Bible Study

Reading and studying the Bible is crucial to our spiritual growth. It is through the Word of God that we learn about His character, His promises, and His plan for our lives. Some practical tips for developing a regular bible study habit include finding a study method that works for you, using a study bible, and incorporating daily reflection and application.

Worship

Worship is a powerful way to connect with God and express our love for Him. It can take many forms, including singing, dancing, or simply reflecting on His goodness. Developing a meaningful worship practice like listening to worship music, and incorporating worship into your daily routine will help deepen your connection and relationship with God.

SERVING OTHERS

As Christians, we are called to serve others and share the love of Christ with those around us. Serving others not only helps us grow in our relationship with God, but it also allows us to make a positive impact in our communities. Some practical tips for finding ways to serve others, include volunteering at a local charity or church, mentoring others, and using our talents and skills to help those in need.

SPIRITUAL DISCIPLINES

In addition to prayer, bible study, worship, and service, there are many other spiritual disciplines that can help us draw closer to God. Some practical ways for incorporating spiritual disciplines into our daily lives and using them to deepen our relationship with God are fasting, silence and solitude, journaling, and practicing gratitude.

Deepening our relationship with God is a lifelong journey that requires intentional effort and commitment. However, with the help of the tips provided in this section, we can develop a deeper and more meaningful relationship with our Creator. As we pray, study the Bible, worship, serve others, and practice spiritual disciplines, we will experience a greater sense of purpose, joy, and fulfillment in our lives. May we all continue to grow in our love for God and our devotion to Him.

Biblical Examples of Forgiveness and its Impact on our Own Life

We will explore several examples of forgiveness in the Bible and the impact it had on the lives of those involved. Through these stories, we will see the transformative power of God's love and the importance of forgiveness in our own lives.

Joseph and His Brothers

The story of Joseph and his brothers is one of the most well-known examples of forgiveness in the Bible. Joseph's brothers sold him into slavery out of jealousy and anger, but years later, Joseph forgave them and even helped them during a time of famine. Through his act of forgiveness, Joseph was able to reconcile with his family and experience the blessings of God's grace.

David and Saul

David was anointed to be king by God, but Saul, the current king, saw him as a threat and sought to kill him. Despite the danger he faced, David refused to harm Saul and instead chose to forgive him.

This act of forgiveness allowed David to remain faithful to God and to eventually become the king of Israel.

Jesus and the Woman Caught in Adultery

In John 8, a woman caught in adultery is brought before Jesus by the Pharisees, who wanted to trap Him. Instead of condemning her, Jesus forgave her and showed her love and compassion. Through this act of forgiveness, the woman was able to experience the transformative power of God's love and was encouraged to sin no more.

Stephen and His Persecutors

Stephen was a follower of Jesus who was stoned to death for his faith. Even as he was being killed, he prayed for his persecutors and forgave them. This act of forgiveness had a profound impact on the early Christian community and inspired others to remain faithful in the face of persecution.

The Prodigal Son

In Luke 15, Jesus tells the story of a prodigal son who squandered his inheritance and returned home in shame. Despite his wrongdoing, his father welcomed him back with open arms and forgave him.

Through this act of forgiveness, the son was able to experience the love and grace of his father and was restored to his family.

Forgiveness is a crucial aspect of the Christian faith and is essential for our spiritual growth and well-being. Through the examples of forgiveness in the Bible, we see the transformative power of God's love and the impact that forgiveness can have on our lives. By choosing to forgive others, we open ourselves up to the blessings of God's grace and can experience true freedom and joy. May we all strive to forgive others as God has forgiven us.

Practical Tips for How to Forgive and Let Go of Past Hurts

We are called to forgive those who have wronged us just as Christ has forgiven us. But forgiving someone who has hurt us deeply is not always easy. It can be a painful and difficult process, but it is essential for our spiritual and emotional health. Here are some practical tips on how to forgive and let go of past hurts, drawing on biblical teachings and psychological insights.

Understanding Forgiveness

The first step in learning how to forgive is to understand what forgiveness is and what it is not. Forgiveness does not mean forgetting or condoning the wrong that was done to us. It does not mean we have to reconcile with the person who hurt us or trust them again. Rather, forgiveness means releasing what we feel toward the person who hurt us and choosing to no longer hold them accountable for their actions. Forgiveness is a decision we make, not a feeling.

Facing Our Emotions

Forgiveness requires us to face and process the emotions that arise from being hurt. It is important to allow ourselves to feel the pain, anger, and sadness that come with being wronged. We need to acknowledge these emotions and express them in healthy ways, such as through prayer, journaling, or talking to a trusted friend or counselor. Ignoring or suppressing our emotions will only prolong the healing process.

Praying for Our Offenders

One of the most powerful ways to forgive is to pray for the person who hurt us. This can be difficult, but it is a way of surrendering our hurt and anger to God and asking Him to heal us and the other person. We can pray for their well-being, for their relationship with God, and for their own healing and growth. As we pray for our offenders, we may find that our hearts soften toward them and we are able to extend grace and compassion.

Setting Boundaries

Forgiveness does not mean we have to continue to tolerate abusive or harmful behavior. It is important to set healthy boundaries with the person who hurt us and to communicate these boundaries clearly. This may mean ending the relationship or limiting contact with the person. Setting boundaries does not mean we are unforgiving; it means we are taking care of ourselves and protecting our well-being.

Letting Go

Forgiveness requires us to let go of the past and move forward. This does not mean we forget what happened. It means we choose to no longer dwell on what happened or allow it to define us. We can release the hurt and pain to God and ask Him to use it for our good and His glory. We can also focus on the positive aspects of our lives and cultivate gratitude and joy.

Forgiving those who have hurt us is not easy, but it is essential for our spiritual and emotional health. By understanding what forgiveness is, facing our emotions, praying for our offenders, setting boundaries, and letting go of the past, we can begin the process of healing and restoration. May God give us the strength and grace to forgive as He has forgiven us.

MOMENTS OF REFLECTION—APPLICATION

In this chapter, we discovered the importance of forgiveness and the freedom it brings to soar in every area of our lives. We are no longer slaves to the pain of our past, but we have become free to embrace a new life and have begun to live with new purpose and prosperity.

What was the hardest offense you had to forgive and why was it so difficult?

What does it mean to live a life of freedom and purpose to you?

What negative feelings were you released from when you experienced forgiveness?

Ask God to help you pray for those who hurt you.

Example: Lord, help me to release (name) from within my heart. Let no bitterness, pain, vengeance, retaliation, or heartache linger from whatever affliction I have suffered from their abuse.

You have to become intentional in seeking God daily in meditation and prayer concerning your direction and assignment.

VALECIA TIGNER, D.D.

Be careful. Do not let your past sneak up on you and remind you of what is no longer true.

CHAPTER FIVE

Overcoming Fear and Anxiety

Do you find yourself overwhelmed by fear and anxiety, unable to fully enjoy the blessings of life? Do you long for peace and freedom but feel trapped by your own thoughts and emotions?

In these pages, we will explore the nature of fear and anxiety, their causes and effects, and most importantly, how to overcome them through the power of faith in Jesus Christ. Drawing from the wisdom of the Bible and the experience of Christian saints and scholars throughout the ages, we will discover practical and effective strategies for dealing with fear and anxiety in all their forms, whether social anxiety, phobias, panic attacks, or general worry.

But this chapter is not only about overcoming fear and anxiety for our own sake. It is also about how our struggles with fear and anxiety can become opportunities for spiritual growth and deeper intimacy with God. We will see how God can use our weaknesses and vulnerabilities to strengthen our faith, refine our character, and equip us to serve others who are struggling with similar challenges.

Fear and anxiety are common experiences in our daily lives. They can arise from various sources such as uncertainty about the future, financial instability, health issues, or personal relationships. As Christians, we have access to powerful tools that can help us overcome fear and anxiety. Through faith in God, prayer, and the teachings of the Bible, we can find peace and comfort in the midst of life's challenges.

This chapter will provide biblical examples of overcoming these obstacles. By finding strength in adversity and trusting in God, we will learn how to navigate challenges in the Christian life and stay strong in our faith.

So, if you are ready to face your fears and embrace a life of courage, hope, and joy, let us begin this journey together. May the Lord guide and bless us as we seek to overcome fear and anxiety and to live the abundant life He has promised.

Overcoming Obstacles

As Christians, we are not exempt from the challenges and obstacles of life. In fact, Jesus warned us that we will face trials and tribulations in this world (John 16:33). However, He also assured us that we can overcome these obstacles because He has already overcome the world. Let's explore some key principles that can help us navigate challenges in the Christian life and overcome obstacles with faith and perseverance.

Trust in God

The most important principle in overcoming obstacles in the Christian life is to trust in God. Proverbs 3:5-6 says, "Trust in the Lord with all your heart and lean not on your own understanding; in all your ways submit to him, and he will make your paths straight." When we face obstacles, it can be easy to rely on our own strength and understanding, but we must remember that God is always with us and He has a plan for our lives. We can trust in Him to guide us through any challenge we may face.

Perseverance

Perseverance is another key principle in navigating challenges in the Christian life. James 1:12 says, "Blessed is the one who perseveres under trial because, having stood the test, that person will receive the crown of life that the Lord has promised to those who love him." When we face obstacles, we must persevere and keep moving forward, even when it is difficult. We can take comfort in knowing that our perseverance will be rewarded in the end.

Prayer

Prayer is a powerful tool in overcoming obstacles in the Christian life. Philippians 4:6-7 says, "Do not be anxious about anything, but in every situation, by prayer and petition, with thanksgiving, present your requests to God. And the peace of God, which transcends all understanding, will guard your hearts and your minds in Christ Jesus." When we face obstacles, we can pray and ask God for help, wisdom, and guidance. He promises to give us the peace we need to face any challenge.

Community

Community is also an important factor in navigating challenges in the Christian life. Ecclesiastes 4:9-10 says, "Two are better than one, because they have a good return for their labor: If either of them falls down, one can help the other up. But pity anyone who falls and has no one to help them up." When we face obstacles, we need the support and encouragement of our Christian brothers and sisters. We can lean on them for guidance, prayer, and practical help.

As we navigate challenges in the Christian life, we can take comfort in knowing that we are not alone. We have a God who loves us and promises to guide us through any obstacle we may face. We also have a community of believers who can support and encourage us along the way. With faith, perseverance, prayer, and community, we can overcome any obstacle and continue to grow in our faith and relationship with God.

The Root Causes of Fear and Anxiety

Fear and anxiety are common experiences that many people face in life. Although fear and anxiety can be normal responses to certain situations, when they become excessive, they can lead to significant distress and interfere with daily activities. As Christians, we are called to trust in God and not be afraid, but sometimes fear and anxiety can get the best of us. Let's discuss the root causes of fear and anxiety.

Lack of Trust in God

The most significant root cause of fear and anxiety for Christians is a lack of trust in God. When we fail to trust in God's plan for our lives, we become anxious and fearful about the future. We forget that God is in control and that He is always with us. We need to remember that God is faithful and will never leave us or forsake us. When we put our trust in Him, we can find peace and comfort in the midst of difficult situations.

Negative Thinking

Another root cause of fear and anxiety is negative thinking. When we focus on negative thoughts, we create a cycle of fear and anxiety that can be hard to break. We need to learn to replace negative thoughts with positive ones. We can do this by focusing on the promises of God and the good things in our lives. We should also practice gratitude and thankfulness, which can help us see things in a more positive light.

Past Trauma and Experiences

Past trauma and experiences can also be a root cause of fear and anxiety. When we have experienced trauma or difficult situations in the past, it can affect how we view the present and the future. We may become fearful or anxious about similar situations happening again. It's important to seek healing and support for past trauma and experiences, whether through counseling or prayer. We need to allow God to heal our past so that we can move forward with peace and confidence.

Lack of Self-Worth

A lack of self-worth can also contribute to fear and anxiety. When we don't believe in ourselves or our abilities, we may become anxious about trying new things or taking risks. We need to remember that we are fearfully and wonderfully made by God and that He has a plan and purpose for our lives. We should focus on our strengths and trust that God will use them for His glory.

Conclusion

Fear and anxiety can be overwhelming, but we have the hope and peace that comes from knowing God. By trusting in Him, focusing on positive thoughts, seeking healing for past trauma, and believing in our self-worth, we can overcome fear and anxiety. Let us remember the words of Philippians 4:6-7, "Do not be anxious about anything, but in everything by prayer and supplication with thanksgiving let your requests be made known to God. And the peace of God, which surpasses all understanding, will guard your hearts and your minds in Christ Jesus."

Examples of Overcoming Fear and Anxiety

The Bible provides us with numerous examples of individuals who faced fear and anxiety but overcame them through faith in God.

David

David, the shepherd boy who became a king, faced numerous challenges throughout his life. In Psalm 23, he writes, "Even though I walk through the darkest valley, I will fear no evil, for you are with me; your rod and your staff, they comfort me." David overcame fear and anxiety by trusting in God's protection and guidance. He knew that God was with him, and this gave him the strength to face any challenge.

Elijah

Elijah was a prophet who faced many difficult situations in his ministry. In 1 Kings 18, he challenged the prophets of Baal to a contest to see whose God was the true God. Despite the opposition he faced, Elijah stood firm in his faith and called upon God to answer by fire. Through this experience, Elijah learned to trust in God's power to overcome fear and anxiety.

PAUL

The Apostle Paul faced numerous trials and difficulties throughout his ministry. In 2 Corinthians 12, he writes about his "thorn in the flesh," a physical ailment that caused him great pain and discomfort. Despite this, Paul writes, "But he said to me, 'My grace is sufficient for you, for my power is made perfect in weakness.'" Paul overcame fear and anxiety by relying on God's grace and strength in his weakness.

JESUS

Of course, the ultimate example of overcoming fear and anxiety is Jesus Christ. In the Garden of Gethsemane, Jesus faced the prospect of his impending crucifixion. He prayed, "Father, if you are willing, take this cup from me; yet not my will, but yours be done." Despite his fear and anxiety, Jesus submitted to God's will and faced his trial with courage and faith.

As Christians, we can learn from these examples and overcome fear and anxiety by trusting in God's protection, power, grace, and will. We can take comfort in the fact that we are not alone in our struggles and that God is always with us. Let us cling to these truths and face our fears with courage and faith.

Finding Strength in Adversity

Life can be unpredictable, and at times, difficult. Unexpected challenges can arise, leaving us feeling helpless and overwhelmed. It's during these moments of adversity that our faith can be tested. As Christians, we believe that God is always with us, but how do we find the strength to endure when we're in the midst of a storm?

One of the most challenging aspects of facing adversity is accepting that we may not understand why it's happening. We may question God's plan and wonder why He would allow us to go through such difficulty. However, as Christians, we know that God has a plan for our lives, even if we can't yet see it.

Jeremiah 29:11 tells us, "For I know the plans I have for you," declares the Lord, "plans to prosper you and not to harm you, plans to give you hope and a future." In times of adversity, it's important to trust in God's plan for us. We may not know what the future holds, but we can trust that God has a purpose for our struggles.

Prayer is a powerful tool for finding comfort and strength during difficult times. When we're facing adversity, it can be easy to feel alone and forgotten. However, we can take comfort in knowing that God is always listening to our prayers.

Philippians 4:6-7 says, "Do not be anxious about anything, but in every situation, by prayer and petition, with thanksgiving, present your requests to God. And the peace of God, which transcends all understanding, will guard your hearts and your minds in Christ Jesus." By bringing our fears and concerns to God in prayer, we can find peace and comfort in His presence.

Let's remember, as Christians, we are not meant to face adversity alone. We are part of a larger community of believers who can offer support and encouragement during difficult times. By drawing on the support of our Christian community, we can find the strength to persevere.

Hebrews 10:24-25 tells us, "And let us consider how we may spur one another on toward love and good deeds, not giving up meeting together, as some are in the habit of doing, but encouraging one another." When we gather with other believers, we can find the strength to keep going and the hope to face the challenges ahead.

Adversity is a part of life, but as Christians, we must have the strength and comfort of our faith to help us through. By trusting in God's plan and finding comfort in prayer, let us hold onto the promise of Isaiah 41:10, "So do not fear, for I am with you; do not be dismayed, for I am your God. I will strengthen you and help you; I will uphold you with my righteous right hand."

Trusting in God

Trusting in God is a fundamental aspect of our faith. It can be challenging to stay strong in our faith, especially during difficult times. However, by leaning on God and trusting in His plan, we can find the strength and encouragement we need to persevere.

To trust in God means to have confidence in Him, to believe that He is faithful, and to rely on Him in all circumstances. Trusting in God requires surrendering control over our lives to Him, acknowledging that He is in charge, and believing that His plans for us are good. Psalm 9:10 says, "Those who know your name trust in you, for you, Lord, have never forsaken those who seek you."

Doubt is a common obstacle that can hinder our ability to trust in God. When doubt creeps in, we need to remind ourselves of God's promises and His faithfulness. Remember the countless times He has come through in the past, and have faith that He will continue to do so in the future. Hebrews 11:1 says, "Now faith is confidence in what we hope for and assurance about what we do not see."

Trusting in God requires seeking His guidance and direction in our lives. Spend time in prayer and reading the Bible, asking God to reveal His plan. Proverbs 3:5-6 says, "Trust in the Lord with all your heart and lean not on your own understanding; in all your ways submit to him, and he will make your paths straight."

When we trust in God, we can find strength in Him even during difficult times. Lean on Him for support and encouragement, knowing that He is with you always. Philippians 4:13 says, "I can do all this through him who gives me strength."

Trusting in God also means resting in His peace. When you feel anxious or worried, turn to God and trust in His peace that surpasses all understanding. Philippians 4:6-7 says, "Do not be anxious about anything, but in every situation, by prayer and petition, with thanksgiving, present your requests to God. And the peace of God, which transcends all understanding, will guard your hearts and your minds in Christ Jesus."

To trust in God requires faith, surrender, and seeking His guidance. When you trust in God, you can find strength, peace, and encouragement to stay strong in your faith. Remember that God is faithful, and He will never forsake you. As you continue to trust in Him, He will guide you and lead you on the path of righteousness.

MOMENTS OF REFLECTION—APPLICATION

Take a moment and invite the peace of God to guard your heart and mind against any challenging thoughts that may arise and leave you feeling overwhelmed and helpless.

You've endured great difficulties and challenges for a reason and perhaps you've questioned the plans of God for your life or wondered why He would allow you to go through such difficulty.

Ask the Lord to strengthen you and show you your community of believers you can draw support from, those who will encourage you to find the strength to persevere.

Spend time in prayer.

TRUST GOD AND BREATHE.

Notes

CHAPTER SIX

The Soaring Life

In a world that often feels weighed down by struggle, stress, and pain, we long for a life that soars above the challenges and hardships we face. As Christians, we know that such a life is possible, but how do we actually live it? How do we soar above the circumstances of our lives and experience the abundant life that Jesus promised?

The answer lies in a deep and abiding relationship with God, one that empowers us to rise above our struggles and find purpose, joy, and fulfillment in Him. In this chapter, we'll explore what it means to live a life that's truly grounded in Christ, one that rises above the noise and distractions of the world and finds its true purpose in Him.

Through biblical insights, personal stories, and practical strategies, we'll discover how to embrace the soaring life that God has called us to and experience the fullness of His love, grace, and power in every area of our lives. Whether you're struggling with anxiety, loneliness, or simply feeling stuck in your faith journey, this chapter offers a powerful vision of what's possible when we surrender our lives to Christ and allow Him to lift us up on wings like eagles.

The soaring life, the journey to freedom and purpose, is not meant to be traveled alone. This chapter will explore the importance of community in the Christian journey, as well as practical tips for building and nurturing meaningful relationships. Using biblical examples and personal stories of community, readers will learn how to soar together through prayer and fellowship.

FREEDOM AND SOARING

Freedom is a concept that is highly valued by people across the world. It is often associated with individual autonomy and the ability to make choices without external constraints. However, for Christians, freedom takes on a deeper meaning that is rooted in our faith.

For Christians, freedom is not just about the ability to make choices, it is also about being set free from the bondage of sin and death. This freedom is made possible through the sacrifice of Jesus Christ on the cross, which has redeemed us from the power of sin and death. As it says in Galatians 5:1, "It is for freedom that Christ has set us free. Stand firm, then, and do not let yourselves be burdened again by a yoke of slavery."

While believers are set free from the power of sin, this does not mean that we are free to do whatever we want. True freedom in Christ is not a license to sin, but it is the ability to live in accordance with God's will. As it says in Galatians 5:13, "You, my brothers and sisters, were called to be free. But do not use your freedom to indulge the flesh; rather, serve one another humbly in love."

Living in freedom means living a life that is pleasing to God and striving to do what is right in His eyes. This involves following His commandments, loving one another, and seeking to serve others. As it says in John 8:36, "So if the son sets you free, you will be free indeed."

Freedom in Christ is a precious gift that has been given to us through the sacrifice of Jesus Christ. As Christians, we should cherish this gift, and strive to live in accordance with God's will. By doing so, we can experience true freedom and live a life that is pleasing to God.

SOARING

Soaring is the act of rising above the challenges and difficulties of life through faith and trust in God. It is a metaphorical reference to the way eagles fly, soaring high above the earth and effortlessly gliding through the sky.

In the same way, as Christians, we are called to rise above the trials and tribulations of this world, relying on our faith to carry us through. Soaring requires us to let go of the things, like fear, doubt, and worry, that hold us down and instead fix our eyes on God and trust in His promises.

Isaiah 40:31 says, "But those who hope in the Lord will renew their strength. They will soar on wings like eagles; they will run and not grow weary, they will walk and not faint." This verse reminds us that when we put our trust in God, He will give us the strength we need to overcome any obstacle and rise above our circumstances.

So, to soar means to live a life of faith, hope, and trust in God, rising above the challenges of this world and experiencing the freedom and joy that comes from a life surrendered to Him.

THE ROLE OF COMMUNITY IN THE JOURNEY TO FREEDOM AND SOARING

From the very beginning, God designed us for community. In Genesis 1:27, we read that God created man and woman in His image, and then commanded them to be fruitful and multiply. This command was not just about procreation, but also about building relationships and community.

In the Christian faith, community plays a vital role in our journey toward freedom and soaring. As believers, we are called to live in fellowship with one another and to support and encourage each other in our faith. This is because God has designed us to be in community, to bear each other's burdens, and to share in each other's joys. By doing so, we can find strength and encouragement in the company of other believers as we seek to live out our faith and grow closer to God.

Throughout the Bible, we see examples of community in action. The early church in Acts 2:42-47 is a perfect example of a community of believers who shared their lives together, devoted themselves to the apostles' teaching, and prayed and worshiped together. The disciples also formed a close-knit community, traveling together and supporting one another through trials and tribulations.

In the journey toward freedom, community can provide a safe and supportive environment for us to share our struggles and receive prayer and encouragement. When we are struggling with sin, addiction, or any other issue, it can be challenging to face it alone. Being part of a community of believers can make all the difference in the world. We can share our struggles with others who have walked similar paths, receive advice, and pray for one another. In this way, we can experience God's healing and freedom together.

Similarly, in the journey toward soaring, community can help us discover and develop our God-given talents and gifts. When we are part of a community that is focused on seeking God's will and fulfilling His purposes, we can discover our unique strengths and abilities. As we work together and support each other, we can accomplish more than we ever could on our own. This can lead to a sense of fulfillment and purpose as we use our gifts to serve others and glorify God.

As Christians, we are called to be part of the body of Christ and to work together toward the common goal of spreading the gospel and making disciples. Through community, we can find the strength, encouragement, and support we need to live out this calling and fulfill God's purposes for our lives. We can learn from the experiences and wisdom of others, receive guidance and correction when we need it, and be accountable to one another. By doing so, we can grow in our faith and become more like Christ.

Community plays a significant role in the journey toward freedom and soaring in the Christian faith. Through fellowship, prayer, and encouragement, we can support each other in our struggles, discover and develop our God-given gifts, and fulfill God's purposes for our lives.

Importance of Community in Achieving Freedom and Soaring

As a Christian, one of the fundamental beliefs is that we are called to live in community with others. Community refers to a group of people who share a common goal, belief, or interest. As Christians, community is vital in achieving freedom and soaring in our spiritual walk. Community plays a critical role in our journey toward freedom and soaring, providing us with the support, encouragement, and accountability that we need to grow and mature in our faith.

This section will explore the reasons why community is crucial and how it can help us live more fulfilling lives.

Support and Encouragement

In a community, we can find support when we need it. Whether we are going through a difficult time or just need someone to talk to, being part of a community means that we have people we can turn to. This support helps us to navigate life's challenges and can make all the difference in our spiritual walk.

Community provides us with the support and encouragement that we need to persevere in our journey toward freedom and soaring. When we face trials and challenges, our community can lift us up in prayer, offer practical assistance, and remind us of God's faithfulness and love.

Accountability and Guidance

Being part of a community means that we have people who hold us accountable. Accountability helps us to stay on track with our spiritual walk and encourages us to live a life that is pleasing to God.

We are not meant to live the Christian life alone; we need others to help us stay accountable and to help us grow.

Community also provides us with accountability and guidance. When we are struggling with sin or temptation, our community can hold us accountable and offer wise counsel and guidance to help us overcome.

Opportunities for Learning and Growth

Community provides us with opportunities for learning and growth. We can learn from one another's experiences, wisdom, and spiritual insights, and grow in our understanding of God's Word and His will for our lives.

Being part of a community means that we can learn from others.

Protection from Isolation and Loneliness

Community provides us with protection from isolation and loneliness. When we are surrounded by a loving and supportive community, we are less likely to fall into despair or to give up on our journey toward freedom and soaring.

Fellowship

Being part of a community allows us to fellowship with like-minded believers. It helps us build relationships, learn from one another, and support each other through life's challenges. Fellowship allows us to share our joys and sorrows, pray for one another, and grow in our faith together.

Breaking Free from Sin and Fear

Sin can hold us back in our spiritual walk. Being part of a community can help us break free from the chains of sin. Our community can hold us accountable, encourage us, and provide support as we seek to live a life that is pleasing to God.

Fear can keep us from stepping out in faith and doing what God has called us to do. Being part of a community can help us overcome our fears. We can find encouragement and support as we step out in faith, and our community can pray for us as we take risks for God.

Using our Gifts

God has given each of us unique gifts and talents. Being part of a community means that we can use these gifts to serve others. We can find opportunities to use our gifts and talents to make a difference in the lives of others.

Being part of a community allows us to fellowship with like-minded believers, be held accountable, find support, break free from sin and fear, learn from others, and use our gifts. As Christians, we are not meant to live the Christian life alone. We need others to help us grow and to support us as we seek to live a life that is pleasing to God.

Christians Making a Difference in the World

As followers of Jesus Christ, we have a responsibility to positively impact the world around us. This can take many forms, such as helping those in need, promoting justice and equality, caring for the environment, spreading the gospel message, and more.

The Bible teaches that Christians are called to be salt and light in the world (Matthew 5:13-16). Salt is a preservative that adds flavor to food, while light illuminates darkness. In the same way, we are called to preserve and add value to the world while shining a light on the truth and goodness of God.

There are countless examples throughout history of Christians who have made a difference in the world, from Mother Teresa's work with the poor in India to William Wilberforce's efforts to abolish slavery in the British Empire. Today, there are still many opportunities for Christians to make a positive impact in their communities and beyond.

As we seek to make a difference in the world, it is important to remember that our ultimate goal is not simply to make the world a better place but to point people to Jesus Christ. We do this by living out our faith with integrity, by sharing the gospel message, and by loving others in a way that reflects the love of Christ.

There are many ways that Christians can make a difference in the world.

Serving Others

Christians are called to love and serve others, especially those who are marginalized and in need. This can take many forms, such as volunteering at a local soup kitchen, visiting the sick or elderly, or advocating for social justice issues.

Sharing the Gospel

Christians are also called to share the good news of Jesus Christ with others and to help others come to a personal relationship with Him. This can involve sharing one's own testimony, engaging in evangelism, or simply living out one's faith in a way that is attractive to others.

BEING A POSITIVE INFLUENCE

Christians can also make a difference in the world by being a positive influence in their communities. This can involve being a good neighbor, being a responsible citizen, and contributing to the common good.

PRAYING FOR OTHERS

Prayer is a powerful tool for making a difference in the world. Christians can pray for individuals, communities, and even nations, asking for God's intervention and guidance.

In all of these ways, Christians can make a positive difference in the world, spreading God's love and compassion to those around them. By following Jesus' example of service and sacrificial love, Christians can truly make an impact on the world around them.

Christians making a difference in the world is about using our God-given gifts, talents, and resources to make a positive impact in the world around us. This can take many forms, but our ultimate goal is to glorify God and share the love of Christ with those around us.

Biblical Examples of Community and How They Relate to Our Lives

The Bible provides many examples of community throughout its pages. These examples can serve as models for how we can live in community with others today, especially as Christians. Here are a few examples and how they relate to our lives:

The early church in Acts — In the book of Acts, we see the early Christian community living together, sharing their possessions, and supporting each other in prayer and worship. They were united in their belief in Jesus and were committed to each other's well-being. Today, we can strive to build similar communities where we support and care for one another as brothers and sisters in Christ.

Ruth and Naomi in the Old Testament — In the book of Ruth, we see a beautiful example of two women who stick together in difficult circumstances. Naomi, an older widow, and her daughter-in-law Ruth, who has also been widowed, travel together and support each other through their grief and hardship. As Christians, we can seek out similar relationships where we support and encourage one another, even in the midst of difficult times.

The parable of the Good Samaritan — In this well-known parable, Jesus teaches us about loving our neighbors as ourselves. The Good Samaritan helps a man who has been beaten and left for dead, even though he is from a different social and ethnic background. Today, we can strive to love and serve others, even if they are different from us, and to be a source of healing and comfort in our communities.

By studying these and other biblical examples of community, we can learn how to build strong relationships with others and live out our faith in practical ways. We can also be encouraged by the fact that we are not alone in our struggles, but are part of a larger community of believers who are journeying together toward a common goal.

SOARING TOGETHER

Soaring Together is a phrase often used to describe the idea of Christians coming together in prayer and fellowship to support and encourage one another. This concept is based on the biblical principle that believers are part of one body with Christ as the head, and that we are called to love and serve one another (1 Corinthians 12:12-27).

Prayer is a crucial aspect of Christian life as it is our direct line of communication with God. Through prayer, we can express our gratitude, confess our sins, ask for guidance, and intercede for others. Prayer is also a powerful tool for building our relationship with God and deepening our faith.

Fellowship, or the act of gathering with other believers, is also essential for spiritual growth. By sharing our experiences and struggles with others, we can gain perspective, encouragement, and support. Fellowship can take many forms, such as attending church services, participating in small group studies, or simply spending time with other believers.

To sum it up, "Soaring Together" in the context of prayer and fellowship means that as believers, we are called to come together to support and encourage one another in our faith journey. Through prayer and fellowship, we can deepen our relationship with God and with each other, and together, we can soar to new heights in our spiritual growth and maturity.

MOMENTS OF REFLECTION—APPLICATION

Isolation is a booby-trap that leads to loneliness and it can trigger us to fall back into a place of negative mindset and despair. This can ultimately lead toward abandonment of goals and to us giving up on our journey toward freedom and soaring.

Take a moment in prayer and ask God to help you to know your community. It's key to soaring to that next level of new life.

- How has being in connection with a church family helped you in your healing process of forgiveness?

- Have you grown as a result of your connection with your community?

- Has your community helped you break free from sin?

- Do you feel a sense of accountability? If so, how?

- Do you have the support you need from your community?

Notes

CHAPTER SEVEN

THE ULTIMATE DESTINATION

The journey to freedom and purpose is not an end in itself. It leads to a life that is anchored in eternity. This chapter will provide a glimpse of heaven and what awaits those who are released to soar. By pressing on and continuing to pursue a life of purpose and freedom, readers will be encouraged to embrace their new life in Christ.

As Christians, we believe that we are on a journey. We have a destination in mind, a place where we will spend eternity in the presence of our Creator. But what is that destination? What does it look like? And how do we get there?

In this chapter, we will explore the concept of the ultimate destination, starting with what the Bible tells us about heaven and hell. We'll examine the characteristics of these places, as well as the experience of those who will dwell there. We'll also delve into the question of how we can be sure that we will end up in the right place, and what we can do to help others find their way there as well.

Throughout this journey, we will be guided by the teachings of Jesus Christ, who is the way, the truth, and the life. We'll see how His life and teachings provide the roadmap for our own journey, and how following His example can help us to reach our ultimate destination.

So, let's get started on this journey together and discover what God has in store for us in the world to come.

THE JOURNEY OF LIFE

The journey of life is an inherently spiritual and meaningful concept that resonates with Christians all over the world. As we navigate through the ups and downs of life, we are on a journey that requires faith, hope, and perseverance to navigate successfully.

The journey of life has a purpose, and as Christians, we believe that God has designed the journey for us with a specific goal in mind. Our journey, therefore, is not just a series of random events but a purposeful path toward fulfilling God's plan for our lives.

As we go through life, it can be easy to lose sight of this purpose and get caught up in the mundane or distracted by worldly pursuits. However, by aligning our journey with God's plan and seeking His guidance, we can find true meaning and purpose in everything we do.

The journey of life is not without its challenges. From personal struggles to external obstacles, we all face difficult times that can test our faith and resilience. However, as Christians, we should believe that God uses these challenges to strengthen and refine us.

In times of trial, it can be tempting to give up or become overwhelmed. However, by relying on God's strength and trusting in His plan, we can overcome any obstacle that comes our way.

The journey of life has a destination, and as Christians, we believe that our ultimate goal is to spend eternity with God in heaven. The Bible teaches us that this destination is only possible through faith in Jesus Christ, who has made a way for us to be reconciled to God.

As we navigate through life, it can be easy to lose sight of this destination and become distracted by worldly pursuits. However, by keeping our eyes fixed on Jesus and looking ahead to the ultimate destination of our journey, we can find the motivation and inspiration we need to stay on track.

While the journey of life can be challenging, it is also a source of great joy and fulfillment. As Christians, we believe that every moment of our journey is an opportunity to grow closer to God and to serve others in love.

By cultivating a spirit of gratitude and contentment, we can find joy and meaning even in the most difficult circumstances.

Life as a Journey Toward a Destination

Life is a journey, and we are all travelers on a road that leads to a destination. As Christians, we believe that our ultimate destination is eternal life with God in heaven. But what does it mean to live life as a journey toward this destination?

It means recognizing that life is not just about the destination but also about the journey itself. Every step we take, every decision we make, and every experience we have is part of the journey. We must learn to appreciate the journey and find joy in it, even when the road is difficult or uncertain.

It means having a clear sense of direction. As travelers, we need a map or a compass to guide us on our journey. For Christians, our map is the Bible, and our compass is the Holy Spirit. We must constantly seek guidance from God to stay on the right path.

It means being prepared for the journey. Just as a traveler must pack the right supplies for a journey, we must prepare ourselves spiritually for the journey of life. This includes developing a strong faith, cultivating a life of prayer, and seeking out a supportive community of fellow travelers.

Lastly, it means staying focused on the destination. Our ultimate goal as Christians is to reach our heavenly home, and we must keep this goal in mind as we journey through life. We must persevere through hardships, resist temptations, and remain faithful to God's plan for our lives.

Life is indeed a journey toward a destination, and as Christians, we have a unique perspective on this journey. By appreciating the journey, seeking direction from God, preparing ourselves spiritually, and staying focused on our ultimate destination, we can live a fulfilling and purposeful life as travelers on the road to eternal life with God.

What the Bible Tell Us about Heaven and Hell

The Bible describes heaven as a place of eternal joy, peace, and bliss where the righteous will dwell with God forever. In the New Testament, Jesus frequently speaks of heaven as a place of great reward for those who follow Him and obey His teachings. In John 14:2-3, Jesus says, "In my Father's house are many mansions: if it were not so, I would have told you. I go to prepare a place for you.

And if I go and prepare a place for you, I will come again, and receive you unto myself; that where I am, there ye may be also."

Heaven is portrayed as a place of great beauty and peace, where there is no pain or suffering. In Revelation 21:4, it says, "He will wipe every tear from their eyes. There will be no more death or mourning or crying or pain, for the old order of things has passed away."

Heaven is also described as a place where believers will be reunited with loved ones who have gone before them. In 1 Thessalonians 4:16-17, it says, "For the Lord himself will come down from heaven, with a loud command, with the voice of the archangel and with the trumpet call of God, and the dead in Christ will rise first. After that, we who are still alive and are left will be caught up together with them in the clouds to meet the Lord in the air. And so we will be with the Lord forever."

HELL

The Bible also speaks of hell as a place of eternal punishment, darkness and separation from God, where there is weeping and gnashing of teeth for those who reject God and His ways. In the New Testament, Jesus often uses the imagery of fire and darkness to describe hell. In Matthew 25:46, Jesus says, "And these shall go away into everlasting punishment: but the righteous into life eternal." He also says in Matthew 25:41, "Depart from me, you who are cursed, into the eternal fire prepared for the devil and his angels."

The Bible teaches that everyone will face judgment after death, and their ultimate destiny will be determined by whether they have accepted Jesus Christ as their Lord and Savior. Those who have accepted Him will go to heaven, while those who have rejected Him will go to hell.

The Bible also emphasizes the importance of choosing to follow God and living a righteous life in order to avoid the eternal consequences of hell. John 3:16-18 says, "For God so loved the world that he gave his one and only Son, that whoever believes in him shall not perish but have eternal life.

For God did not send his Son into the world to condemn the world, but to save the world through him. Whoever believes in him is not condemned, but whoever does not believe stands condemned already because they have not believed in the name of God's one and only Son."

THE ROADMAP TO HEAVEN

The roadmap to heaven is the steps and guidance outlined in the Bible that can help believers journey toward their ultimate destination, which is eternal life with God in heaven.

According to Christian belief, humans were created by God to have a relationship with Him, but sin has separated us from Him. However, God loves us and desires for us to be reconciled to Him. To achieve this, He sent His son, Jesus Christ, to die on the cross for our sins and rise again, so that we may have eternal life through faith in Him.

The Bible provides guidance on how we can follow Jesus and live a life that is pleasing to God. It outlines the steps we need to take, such as believing in Jesus, repenting of our sins, following God's commands, staying connected to Him through prayer and worship, and sharing the good news with others.

As Christians, we believe that our ultimate destination is heaven where we will spend eternity with God. However, the journey to heaven can be long and difficult. We may encounter many obstacles and challenges along the way, and it can be easy to lose our sense of direction.

The roadmap to heaven, therefore, is a guide for believers to navigate the challenges of life and stay on course toward their ultimate destination. It is not a guarantee of an easy journey, but rather a roadmap that helps believers stay focused on their relationship with God and His purpose for their lives. By following the roadmap to heaven, Christians can experience the joy, peace, and fulfillment that come from living a life that is centered on God and His will.

Fortunately, God has given us a roadmap to heaven — the Bible. In His book, we can find guidance, wisdom, and encouragement for our journey.

Here are some key steps to follow on the roadmap to heaven:

Believe in Jesus Christ. The first step on the roadmap to heaven is to believe in Jesus Christ as our Lord and Savior. This means accepting that He died on the cross for our sins and rose again, and that through Him, we can have eternal life.

Repent of our sins. Once we believe in Jesus, we must repent of our sins and ask for forgiveness. This means acknowledging the ways we have fallen short of God's standards and committing to turn away from sin.

Follow God's commands. As we journey toward heaven, we must seek to follow God's commands as outlined in the Bible. This includes loving God with all our heart, soul, and mind, and loving our neighbors as ourselves.

Stay connected to God through prayer and worship. Prayer and worship are essential components of our journey to heaven. Through prayer, we can communicate with God and seek His guidance, while worship allows us to praise and honor Him.

Share the good news with others. Finally, as we travel the roadmap to heaven, we should share the good news of Jesus Christ with others. This means telling them about God's love and the hope we have in Him.

The roadmap to heaven may not always be easy, but it is a journey worth taking. By following these steps and relying on the guidance of the Bible, we can stay on course and reach our ultimate destination which is eternal life with God in heaven.

A Glimpse of Heaven

Heaven is a place of unimaginable beauty and joy that awaits those who are released to soar. It is a place where pain and suffering are no more, and where God's love and presence are felt in every moment.

Heaven is a place of perfection, where everything is as it is meant to be. The Bible describes it as a place where there is no more death, sorrow, or crying. It is a place of eternal life where believers will be reunited with loved ones who have gone before them. In heaven, we will also have glorified bodies that are free from sickness, pain, and imperfection.

One of the most amazing aspects of heaven is the presence of God. In heaven, we will see God face-to-face, and we will know Him fully as we are fully known. We will be able to worship Him without any distractions, and we will experience a level of intimacy with Him that we cannot even begin to imagine.

Heaven is a place of joy, and there are many things that will bring us joy in heaven. We will experience the joy of fellowship with God and with other believers. We will also have the joy of exploring the new heavens and new earth, which God has prepared for us. There will be no more sin, pain, or suffering, and we will be free to enjoy all of God's blessings without any hindrances.

While we cannot earn our way into heaven, there are things we can do to prepare ourselves for the joys that await us. We can cultivate a deeper relationship with God through prayer, bible study, and worship. We can also seek to live a life of obedience to God's Word, and we can share the love of Christ with others.

As we look forward to this glorious future, let us seek to live a life that is pleasing to God and that prepares us for the joys that await us in heaven. May we always remember that our true home is not here on earth, but in the heavenly realms where we will one day be with our Lord and Savior, Jesus Christ.

The Joy of Homecoming

As Christians, we understand that this world is not our permanent home. We are sojourners on this earth, and our final destination is our eternal home with God. While we journey through life, we encounter trials, difficulties, and setbacks that can sometimes leave us feeling discouraged, overwhelmed, and weary. But the good news is that no matter how far we may wander, we can always come back home to the loving arms of our heavenly Father.

The term "homecoming" can mean different things to different people. For some, it may refer to returning to their place of birth or childhood home. For others, it may mean a reunion with loved ones who have been separated for a long time. But for Christians, homecoming refers to our return to God, our creator and redeemer. It is a spiritual journey that begins with acknowledging our need for God's forgiveness and grace and culminates in our eternal home in heaven.

The story of the prodigal son in Luke 15:11-32 is a beautiful illustration of the joy of homecoming. It tells the story of a young man who leaves his father's home, squanders his inheritance on wild living, and ends up destitute. In the end, he realizes the error of his ways and decides to return to his father's home where he is warmly welcomed and embraced by his father. This story teaches us that no matter how far we may stray from God, He is always waiting for us with open arms. The joy of homecoming is not just about our return to God, but it is also about experiencing His unconditional love, forgiveness, and acceptance.

The road to homecoming is not always easy. It requires us to take an honest look at ourselves, acknowledge our weaknesses, and turn away from our sin. As we journey toward home, we may face opposition, temptation, and spiritual warfare, but we can take heart in the promise that God is with us every step of the way.

The joy of homecoming is multifaceted. It is the joy of being reunited with our heavenly Father, the joy of experiencing His love and forgiveness, the joy of being part of the family of God, and the joy of knowing that our ultimate destiny is secure. Homecoming also brings with it a sense of peace, contentment, and purpose. As we abide in Christ and walk in His ways, we experience the fullness of joy that only He can provide.

The joy of homecoming is a profound and life-changing experience for Christians. It is the assurance that no matter how far we may wander, we can always come back home to God. As we journey toward our eternal home, we can take comfort in the knowledge that we are not alone, and that God is always with us. May the joy of homecoming be a reality in our lives as we seek to live for Him and serve Him faithfully.

Embracing Your New Life in Christ

When we accept Jesus Christ as our Lord and Savior, we are born again and become a new creation. Our old life is gone, and we are given a new life in Christ. This new life in Christ is a gift of grace, and it comes with many benefits, including eternal life, forgiveness of sins, and the indwelling of the Holy Spirit. However, embracing this new life can be challenging, especially if we are accustomed to living according to the ways of the world.

The first step in embracing our new life in Christ is to understand our new identity. The Bible teaches we are now children of God. We are identified by our relationship with Christ. This means that we are no longer condemned but are now free from the power of sin. As we embrace our new identity in Christ, we begin to see ourselves and others differently.

Embracing our new life in Christ requires us to grow in our relationship with Him. This means that we must spend time in prayer and fellowship with Him. We must also be intentional about seeking His will and obeying His commands. As we grow in our relationship with Christ, we begin to see His hand at work in our lives, and we become more confident in our faith.

A significant way we can embrace our new life in Christ is by sharing our faith with others. Jesus commands us to go and make disciples of all nations, and this command extends to all believers. Sharing our faith with others can be challenging, but it is essential in fulfilling God's plan for our lives. As we share our faith, we not only help others to come to know Christ, we also grow in our own faith.

Living according to God's Word is also essential in embracing our new life in Christ. The Bible is our guide for living, and it provides us with the wisdom and strength we need to walk in faith. As we study God's Word, we begin to understand His character and His will for our lives. This understanding helps us to make better choices and to live according to His plan.

Embracing our new life in Christ is a journey that requires faith, obedience, and perseverance. As we seek to understand our new identity in Christ, live according to God's Word, grow in our relationship with Him, and share our faith with others, we will experience the fullness of life that Christ promises. May we all embrace our new life in Christ and live each day for His glory.

THE SOARING LIFE: BECAUSE FREEDOM IS BEAUTIFUL

Two years after my initial sermon, I was licensed and ordained in my pastoral position. Shortly after that, in the living room of my two bedroom apartment, my church was born. My roommate and I faithfully set up fifteen rented chairs every Saturday night for Sunday morning services.

Six months later, while on my way to visit a sick member, I drove past a vacant bank building with a for rent sign in the yard. I found myself pulling into the parking lot. I jotted down the number and the rest was history. Four months later, we were moving in, and we ended up buying the building. God has always been faithful and true to His promises.

I attended bible college in early 2000, and recently received an honorary doctorate degree in Theology. Now I have two degrees. I've been invited on TBN to give my testimony. I've received invitations to preach and to sing. God began using me in the area of demonic deliverance. The power of God was manifesting stronger and stronger in my life. Everyone could sense His presence manifesting through my preaching and prayers when I ministered. People were healed and delivered from illnesses or demonic oppression and even demon possession. It was mind blowing. I also began to operate in prophetic gifting as well.

Every round went higher and higher. When I thought I couldn't go any higher or there wasn't anything else God could do with me, or rather pull out of me, He did.

So here I am, years later living a life of freedom and renewal, what I call the soaring life.

I am a woman of many layers. I have many labels:

- I am a pastor (twenty-six years and counting)

- Motivational Speaker

- Deliverance Minister

- Psalmist

- Prophetess

- Mentor

- Entrepreneur
- Author

Keep believing in yourself. But most of all, keep believing in Him and you too will be released to soar.

Freedom is Beautiful!

Moments of Reflection — Application

Prayer of Salvation

Father God, I thank You for who You are and all that You are. I humbly submit my life to You. I confess with my mouth that Jesus Christ is Lord, and I believe in my heart that You have raised Jesus from the dead (Rom. 10:9). I believe that Jesus is now seated with You in heavenly places and will intercede on my behalf (Eph.1:20, Rom. 8:34). Please forgive me of all my sins and cleanse me of all unrighteousness.

I thank You, Lord, that I am now a new creature in Christ Jesus (2 Cor. 5:17). Thank You for creating in me a clean heart and renewing a right spirit within me (Psalm 51:10). I thank You that I am now Your child and as such entitled to all of the blessings and benefits that accompany salvation (Psalm 103).

Thank You, my Father God, for healing, wholeness and restoration in EVERY area of my life.

In Jesus' Mighty Name,

AMEN

Notes

CONCLUSION

Released to Soar is a compelling Christian book that offers readers an insightful journey toward spiritual growth, freedom, and fulfillment. Throughout the book, we have been presented with powerful insights, practical strategies, and inspiring stories that will help us break free from the limitations of the past and embrace a life of purpose, joy, and abundance. As we reach the end of this transformative journey, it is essential to reflect on the significant lessons we have learned and the impact they can have on our lives.

One of the core messages of *Released to Soar* is that we are all created with a unique purpose and destiny, and we have the power to fulfill that destiny. You have been encouraged to let go of our fears, doubts, and insecurities and to trust God's plan for our lives. By doing so, we can tap into our God-given potential and soar to new heights.

Another key takeaway from *Released to Soar* is the importance of forgiveness. The book reminds us that holding onto grudges, bitterness, and resentment only holds us back from experiencing the fullness of God's love and grace. Through forgiveness, we can release the pain of the past and move forward with a renewed sense of purpose and freedom.

Released to Soar also emphasizes the power of prayer and the role it plays in our spiritual growth. Readers are encouraged to develop a consistent prayer life, seeking God's guidance and wisdom every day. By doing so, we can tap into the supernatural power of God and experience His presence in our lives.

As we conclude this transformative journey, it is important to remember that our transformation does not end with the final page of this book. Rather, it is just the beginning of a lifelong journey toward spiritual growth and fulfillment. We must continue to apply the lessons we have learned and strive toward a deeper relationship with God.

May you be inspired and motivated to take bold steps toward your God-given purpose. You are a unique and valuable creation of God, and you have been created to fulfill a specific purpose in His kingdom. It is time to break free from the limitations that have held you back and step into the fullness of your destiny.

Another key theme we have explored in this book is the importance of faith. Faith is the foundation of our relationship with God, and it is the key that unlocks the door to our destiny. Without faith, it is impossible to please God, and without faith, we will never experience the fullness of what God has in store for us.

Faith is not just a feeling or an emotion. It is a choice that we make to believe in the promises of God even when everything around us seems to be falling apart. It is a choice to trust in His goodness and His faithfulness even when we cannot see the way ahead.

Another key theme that we have explored in this book is the power of prayer. Prayer is not just a religious ritual. It is a powerful tool that God has given us to communicate with Him and to access His supernatural power. When we pray, we invite God into our situations, and we allow Him to work on our behalf.

Prayer is not just about asking God for things; it is also about spending time in His presence and building a deeper relationship with Him. When we cultivate a habit of prayer, we open ourselves up to a whole new realm of possibilities, and we position ourselves to receive the blessings that God has in store for us.

Finally, as we wrap up this book, I want to remind you that you are not alone on this journey. God is with you every step of the way, and He has given you the Holy Spirit to guide and empower you. You are surrounded by a cloud of witnesses, both in heaven and on earth, who are cheering you on and praying for you.

So, my friend, it is time to spread your wings and soar to new heights in your faith. It is time to step out in faith, trusting in God's promises and His faithfulness. It is time to cultivate a habit of prayer and spend time in His presence, allowing Him to lead and guide you.

Remember, you are not just released to fly, you are released to soar! May you continue to walk in the freedom and power that God has given you, and may you fulfill your God-given purpose in His Kingdom.

ABOUT THE AUTHOR

Dr. Valecia Tigner, D.D. is a writer, mentor, inspirational speaker, coach, and pastor.

Apostle Tigner's ministry started as a Bible study group, over twenty-six years ago. This study group unexpectedly transitioned into a church, and Resurrected Life Christian Fellowship Ministry (RLCFM) was born, with her being the pastor. Apostle Tigner carries the message of Deliverance. She's anointed in demon deliverance, leading spiritual warfare prayers, and diligently teaching GOD's word. Apostle Tigner's ministry impacts lives globally through the prophetic work of the Holy Spirit.

Apostle Tigner teaches online courses surrounding the topics of Deliverance and Bondage Breaking. She is featured in two published books, where she wrote the Prayer.

VALECIA TIGNER, D.D.

Apostle Tigner has a love for people, and GOD's desire for them to be free.... "Because Freedom is Beautiful"

www.ingramcontent.com/pod-product-compliance
Lightning Source LLC
Chambersburg PA
CBHW071125090426
42736CB00012B/2010